AMISH CANNIN PRESERVING COOKBOOK

350+ The Complete Delicious Waterbath Canning And Preserving Recipes, Including How To Make Jams, Jellies, Fruits, Sauces, Chutneys, Marinades, Curds And More

BY: WALLACE A. TROTTER TROTTER

TABLE OF CONTENTS
INTRODUCTIONS
RECIPES

WHY MAKE JAM? 12

CHOOSING YOUR INGREDIENTS 12

    Food for free 13
    Fruit and pectin 13

PRESERVING EQUIPMENT 13

    THE JARS 14
    OTHER SPECIAL EQUIPMENT 14
    PRESERVING PAN 14
    DOUBLE BOILER 15
    FOOD MILL 15
    JAR FUNNEL 15
    JAR LIFTER 15
    JAM THERMOMETER 15
    JELLY BAG 15
    MUSLIN 15
    SEALING 16
    LABELS 16

PRESERVING TECHNIQUES 16

    JAM: THE TRADITIONAL METHOD 16
    COOKING THE FRUIT 16
    ADDING THE SUGAR 16
    BOILING THE JAM 17
    TESTING FOR SETTING POINT 17
    The cold plate test 17
    Using a jam thermometer 17
    The flake test 17
    SKIMMING 18
    DISPERSING THE FRUIT 18
    FILLING AND STORING 18
    JAM: THE MACERATING METHOD 18
    MAKING MARMALADE 19
    POACHING 19
    PARING THE RIND FIRST 19
    MAKING JELLIES 20
    MAKING CURDS 20

MAKING CHUTNEYS AND PICKLES	21
PICKLING VINEGAR	21
SWEET PICKLING VINEGAR	22
MAKING NECTARS AND SYRUPS	22
KEEPING TIMES	23
PROBLEM-SOLVING	23
WHY JAM GOES MOLDY	23
WHY TINY BUBBLES APPEAR	23
WHY FRUIT RISES IN THE JAM	23
WHY JAM CRYSTALLIZES	24
WHY JAM WON'T SET	24
WHY JAM SHRINKS IN THE JAR	24

JAMS 24

SPICED BLACKBERRY & NECTARINE JAM	25
APRICOT JAM	26
APRICOT & VANILLA JAM	27
WHITE CURRANT & RED CHILI JAM	27
RASPBERRY JAM	28
STRAWBERRY & GOOSEBERRY JAM	29
STRAWBERRY & VANILLA JAM	29
PLUM JAM	30
DAMSON JAM	30
PLUM & MARROW SQUASH JAM	31
EVERY & RASPBERRY JAM	31
CHERRY JAM	32
COUNTRYSIDE JAM	33
PEAR & VANILLA JAM	33
RHUBARB & APRICOT JAM	34
RHUBARB & LIME JAM	35
GREEN FIG JAM	35
FIG & PEAR JAM	36
GREEN TOMATO JAM	36
GREEN TOMATO & ANGELICA JAM	37
TUTTI FRUTTI JAM	37
GOOSEBERRY JAM	38
GOOSEBERRY & ELDERFLOWER JAM	38
EVERY & PEAR JAM	39
DUMPSIDEARY JAM	40

JELLIES 40

RED CURRANT & GOOSEBERRY JELLY	41
ROSE HIP JELLY	42
ROWAN JELLY	42

- CRAB APPLE JELLY 42
- DAMSON & APPLE JELLY 43
- SLOE & APPLE JELLY 44
- BLACKBERRY JELLY 44
- RASPBERRY JELLY 45

MARMALADES 45

- APPLE & BLACK CURRANT MARMALADE 45
- APPLE & CRANBERRY MARMALADE 46
- SEVILLE ORANGE MARMALADE 46
- LEMON & FIG MARMALADE 47
- LIME MARMALADE 48
- EVERY MARMALADE 48
- EVERY & VANILLA MARMALADE 49
- QUINCE & ORANGE MARMALADE 49

FRUITS IN SYRUP 50

- APRICOTS IN SYRUP 51
- NECTARINES IN SYRUP 51
- DAMSONS IN SYRUP 51
- FIGS IN VANILLA SYRUP 52
- ORANGE SLICES IN SPICED HONEY 53
- WHOLE PEACHES IN BRANDY 53
- GREENGAGES IN BRANDY 54
- CHERRIES IN EAU DE VIE 54

FRUITS 55

- Preserving Fruit 55
- Canning Fruit 55
- APPLESAUCE 55
- BLUEBERRY PIE FILLING 56
- CHERRY PIE FILLING 57
- APPLE PIE FILLING 57
- FRUIT PUDDING 58

CHUTNEYS 58

- APRICOT CHUTNEY 59
- APRICOT & ORANGE CHUTNEY 59
- BEET CHUTNEY 60
- VEGETABLE GARDEN CHUTNEY 60
- DAMSON CHUTNEY 61
- GREEN TOMATO & RED ONION CHUTNEY 62
- MANGO CHUTNEY 63
- NECTARINE CHUTNEY 64

- EVERY CHUTNEY 64
- ONION MARMALADE 64
- RED TOMATO & GARLIC CHUTNEY 65
- HOT TOMATO, APPLE, & CHILI CHUTNEY 66
- AUNT EDNA'S APPLE CHUTNEY 66
- APPLE & DATE CHUTNEY 67
- PUMPKIN CHUTNEY 68
- MARROW SQUASH CHUTNEY 68
- PEAR CHUTNEY 69

CURDS 69

- CRAB APPLE & VANILLA CURD 69
- APRICOT CURD 70
- RASPBERRY CURD 71
- BLUEBERRY & LIME CURD 72
- GOOSEBERRY CURD 72
- LEMON CURD 73
- BITTER ORANGE CURD 73
- GRAPEFRUIT CURD 74
- BUTTERNUT & GINGER CURD 74

TOMATOES 75

- STEWED TOMATOES 75
- HOT SAUCE 75
- TOMATO SOUP 76
- CHILI BASE 77
- (BASIC) TOMATO JUICE 77
- SEASONED TOMATO JUICE 78
- HOMEMADE V-8 JUICE 78
- PIZZA SAUCE (VARIATION 1) 78
- PIZZA SAUCE (VARIATION 2) 79
- PIZZA SAUCE (VARIATION 3) 80
- KETCHUP (VARIATION 1) 80
- KETCHUP (VARIATION 2) 81
- SALSA (VARIATION 1) 82
- SALSA (VARIATION 2) 82

PICKLES 83

- SPICED CRAB APPLE PICKLE 83
- PICKLED PEARS 84
- MOSTARDA DI FRUTTA 85
- PICKLED DAMSONS 86
- PICKLED APRICOTS 87
- PRESERVED LEMONS 87

- PICCALILLI 88
- PICKLED SHALLOTS 89
- SWEET & SOUR ONIONS 90
- SWEET KOSHER DILL PICKLES 90
- BREAD-AND-BUTTER PICKLES 91
- MUSTARD PICKLES 92
- SWEET DILL PICKLES 93
- BANANA PICKLES 94
- REFRIGERATOR PICKLES 95

PICKLED VEGETABLES 96
- CRISP DILLY GREEN BEANS 96
- PICKLED BEETS 97
- HARVARD BEETS 98

CHEESE 99
- Schmierkase 100
- Cottage Cheese 100
- Egg Cheese 101
- Cup of Cheese 101

BEVERAGES 102
- Fresh Meadow Tea 102
- Frozen Meadow Tea Concentrate 103
- Root Beer 103
- Lemonade 104
- Grape Juice Concentrate 104
- Eggnog 105
- Peppermint Drink 105
- Tomato Juice Cocktail 106
- Spiced Cider 106

PUDDINGS, DUMPLINGS, AND DESSERTS 107
- Vanilla Cornstarch Pudding 108
- Chocolate Cornstarch Pudding 108
- Cracker Pudding 109
- Graham Cracker Pudding 109
- Banana Pudding 110
- Tapioca Pudding 110
- Apple Dumplings 111
- Apple Rolls 112
- Syrup 112
- Baked Apples 113
- Baked Egg Custard 113

    Caramel Pudding 114
    Cottage Pudding 114
    Date Pudding 115

RELISHES 116
    GREEN TOMATO RELISH 116
    ONION RELISH 117
    PEPPER RELISH 117
    PICKLE RELISH 118
    ZUCCHINI RELISH 118

THE CONCLUSION 120

INTRODUCTIONS

Canning and preserving were always a part of family life for me as an Amish child growing up as the eldest girl in a family of seven. They were a summertime custom that complemented gardening. Despite having four boys and a huge garden growing up, I still consider canning and preserving part of my summer tradition. Another heritage of my love for gardening is keeping my garden looking beautiful.

Even while canning and preserving require some work, you may benefit from your winter labor with the right equipment and a little time in the kitchen. You succeed greatly when you place your shining jars on shelves or cupboards and realize your work was responsible for making them there. For me, it knows exactly what's in those jars. The only artificial product I use is fresh food from my garden. I still purchase fruit from surrounding orchards because we don't have any fruit trees, but that's okay because I still know where the food comes from.

While you might need a few things, most are inexpensive and versatile. I suggest purchasing new jars for your first batch of canning. If you do it this way, you may be sure there are no chips or fractures on the jar's body. Pots with cracked or chipped external edges won't create a solid seal.

Jars in quart, pint, and half-pint sizes are all readily available. Jelly jars are another option; they are much smaller and hold about a half cup. I use quart-sized jars to preserve everything I can, including pickles, applesauce, peaches, pears, beets, and tomato juice. Even though my family of six consumes a lot of food at every meal, I still store my jams, sauces, salsas, and relishes in pint-sized jars. You can use any jar size that is practical for your family.

New canning jars—often known as mason jars—come with lids and rings, also called screw bands. During the canning process, flat caps feature an inner rubber rim that fits the top of the glass jar and creates a tight seal, keeping your food fresh. Covers usually are only used once and are available for separate purchases. Unlike pots, which endure forever, screw bands must be replaced when worn out because they occasionally rust and get bent.

The dishes in this cookbook are made in a pot of boiling water. You can also use a pressure canner, but I needed to be more confident suggesting it in my book because I don't own one and haven't used one. I always had success with water-bath canning instead. It would help to have a canner, preferably a hot-water bath canner. If you already own a canner, which is just a large stockpot, purchasing another one is unnecessary. My 12-quart stainless-steel kettle frequently serves as a canner.

You must frequently take your jars from hot water when canning, so you must have a jar lifter.

Even though unnecessary, a canning funnel is recommended, especially when preserving sauces or fruits. Since they won't melt or get soiled, I prefer horns made of stainless steel.

A canning rack is also suggested to keep your jars off the bottom of the kettle and away from direct heat. You can make your frame by tying screw bands or using a cake cooling rack with a pot instead of a canner. I've substituted a clean dishcloth in a pinch for my canning rack. It stops the jars from shattering and banging as they heat up.

Before filling your jars, it's essential to warm them up; this won't sterilize them because that will happen throughout the canning process; instead, it will help to lessen the discomfort of a sudden temperature change. The best method for warming them is with hot water. Before processing them in your canner, some counsel suggested bringing them to a simmer (180°F, almost boiling) in water. You can also use your dishwasher, but I've found that washing my jars in hot, soapy water and letting them dry on the counter works just as well to maintain their heat. However, my kitchen is consistently warm throughout the summer since I don't have air conditioning.

It has always worked for me to put the lids on hot jars before placing them in a canner with boiling water, but if you're concerned that your pots won't seal in the canner, you can also heat the lids in the same manner as the jars. The banks don't need to be heated because the screw bands are fastened before you put them in the canner.

When filling the jars, follow every recipe's instructions for the headspace or the distance between the jar's top and the food's top. Sticky foods like canned fruit or applesauce can create a mess if the pots are overstuffed. Although they require a little less space than other recipes, soft jams or fruit liquids still require around a half-inch.

After putting the food within the jars, clean the surface thoroughly to remove any food crumbs or residue, paying particular attention to the outside rim. This step must be completed appropriately for the canning process to produce a tight seal.

Place your filled jars in the canner, raise or lower the water level until all jars are submerged, and screw the bands on just the fingertip tight (do not use a tool or device to tighten them). The procedure is carried out as directed in the recipe at a full rolling boil. Once they are completed, carefully remove the jars using the jar lifter. Wait to move them for 24 hours after setting them down on a sturdy place like your kitchen counter. Now is no time to dry the pots or take the screw bands off. You can remove the bars after 24 hours, check the jars for a good seal, and clean them.

After placing them in the refrigerator, eat the contents of any unsealed jars as soon as possible. Whether this raises food safety concerns depends on what is being canned; for instance, you do not want to eat chicken soup that has been sitting at room temperature for at least 24 hours.

Keep your jars in a perfect, enclosed space, such as a pantry, cupboard, or basement. Canning is a fantastic option because the temperature in basement storage is typically colder and more consistent.

Home-canned food is frequently safe to eat for a year. I've successfully stored food for up to two years. However, the taste could be better. Every canned food must be marked with dates to facilitate speedy usage. If mold or discoloration develops in the jar, the food is no longer safe to consume. All unsealed food that isn't consumed right away needs to be refrigerated. Like fresh food, once the vacuum seal has been broken, the food can degrade quickly.

I hope you like this book and all the products of your labor.

REGARDING YIELDS:

In my experience, many canning recipe yields are only estimates. Please remember that the yield will sometimes match the amount specified in the recipe because it's hard to forecast how many quarts, pints, etc., you'll get from a single dish.

REGARDING THE RECIPES:

Every summer, my extended family and I still utilize the recipes in this book to preserve the produce from our gardens. I hope you enjoy them and employ them frequently, as I do.

....ORDER RIGHT NOW

WHY MAKE JAM?

Opening a pantry or food cabinet and seeing shelves packed with vibrant jars of handmade preserves is fulfilling. When a generous smear of strawberry jam on your bread conjures images of longer, warmer, lighter days, these summer and fall flavors may be needed to brighten the mood on a gloomy, dark winter. Making preserves, for me, is all about preserving the taste of the fruit or vegetable, no matter what it is, in a jar for later use.

I've been making jam for around 30 years, and despite making plenty of sticky mistakes, I've always enjoyed it. It is a customary aspect of homemaking that honors the changing of the seasons and, in some way, improves the quality of living. My preserves are unlike anything you can buy in a shop because they are homemade and packed with significant bits. Rarely are the aromas of the fruits covered up with spices; they come through clearly. I cut back on the sugar whenever possible because the results taste better when the fruits are sourer.

Making preserves has never been more popular, especially in the present context of worries about reducing waste, logging fewer food miles, and eating seasonally and locally sourced food.

CHOOSING YOUR INGREDIENTS

Nothing compares to the flavor of a homegrown strawberry that has just been picked after ripening in the sun and being grown in your garden. Strawberries, to give just one example, can now be purchased practically all year round, thanks to new varieties, the use of field tunnels, and the massive increase in imported produce. This flavor, which is quite sweet and potent, can be preserved in preserves.

It's difficult to beat using your homegrown produce for canning because the components will be fresh, and you'll have control over the growing environment.

Another excellent resource is farmers' markets. You'll be able to tell that the fruit and vegetables were grown nearby, and you'll have a better chance of finding uncommon types. Rinse produce before using, regardless of where it came from, but preferably avoid washing bush fruits because doing so can lessen their juice quality. However, you must rinse and drain them if you suspect they were sprayed.

FOOD FOR FREE

Sometimes all you need to do is go out and look for the ingredients; they may already be there. Assuming you know what to look for, you can find plenty of edible fruits and berries in woodlands and hedgerows (if you live in a region of the nation where these are plentiful). Crab apples, damsons, greengages, and blackberries can grow wild. Alternately, if you know someone who produces more fruit than they can consume, offer to buy it from them in exchange for a jar of fruit preserve. It benefits both parties.

FRUIT AND PECTIN

To get the right amount of pectin in almost all fruit preserves, you must select fresh, high-quality fruit that is just ripe. This is so that jam can adequately set, which requires the proper ratio of pectin, acid, and sugar. Pectin level varies among fruits, with just-ripe fruit having a higher pectin content. Crab apples, Seville oranges, damsons, gooseberries, quinces, and currants are among the fruits that are high in pectin. Strawberries, pears, elderberries, fresh apricots, and cherries are some fruits low in pectin. Some fruits have a shallow pectin content, so jams created from these fruits will require additional assistance to set. Fruit that is too ripe can also have less pectin, making it unsuitable for jam-making. However, it is appropriate for nectars, so you may make lovely nectar or syrup out of any fruit that is too ripe for jam.

There are several strategies to increase the pectin content. In mixed-fruit jams, the higher pectin content of one fruit can be utilized to balance out the lower pectin level of another; alternatively, bottled pectin or lemon juice can be used at a rate of 1-2 lemons per 4 pounds of fruit.

PRESERVING EQUIPMENT

The guiding principle behind all preservation forms is preventing deterioration brought on by the development of yeast, mold, and bacteria. These microorganisms are eliminated when heated to temperatures high enough to sterilize them. Once fixed, preserves must be tightly sealed so air cannot get inside. Jams with less sugar must be consumed more rapidly because preserves with 60 percent or more sugar are less likely to support yeast growth.

THE JARS

Mason jars are the most frequently used for preserving food in the United States. To help establish a tight seal, they contain a screw-on cover comprising two or more portions. Also available are canning jars in the European design, with a glass top and a robust wire clamp. Various sizes are available for both types.

Additionally, reused jam or other condiment jars are an option. But make sure the jars are intact and free of fractures and that the lids are tight. Make sure the lids won't rust. Corrosive substances shouldn't come in contact with the preserve, mainly if it contains vinegar (as in chutneys and pickles).

The jars must be sterilized, and I like the straightforward procedure described here. The jars should be washed in soapy water, rinsed with hot water, and dried by air. Lay the pots on their sides on a folded dish towel on an oven shelf. Heat the oven to 225°F a little before you need to use them, then leave the jars there for 30 minutes. When you pour the hot jam into the jars, they should still be warm.

OTHER SPECIAL EQUIPMENT

THERE ARE A FEW ITEMS YOU CAN BUY FOR PRESERVATION:

PRESERVING PAN

A fantastic investment is a large, nonreactive, noncorrosive preserving pan that can contain a lot of boiling jam. When brought back up to the set point, this pan is wide and shallow to promote quick evaporation. Any preserve won't burn because a high-quality pan will have a hefty, thick base. Although copper and aluminum pans are standard, stainless steel is preferable and unquestionably required for preparing preserves with vinegar.

Never overfill the pan since the jam rises as it comes to a rolling boil. If the pan is too small and too full, you will either have an overflowing mess of boiling syrupy jam, or you won't be able to raise the temperature high enough for every setting point to prevent this from happening.

DOUBLE BOILER

This can be substituted by a bowl put over a pan of simmering water, but it is still valid when producing fruit curds, syrups, and nectars.

FOOD MILL

Fruit can be sieved to extract the purée, which is ideal for producing jams and has a nice texture, using a good-quality food mill with many disks of varying degrees of coarseness. Apples can be puréed without first being peeled and cored.

JAR FUNNEL

This is crucial for safely ladling hot jam into jars. Select one wide enough to prevent jamming with fruit bits and tiny sufficient to fit into most of your pots. The funnel and the jars should be heated and sterilized in the oven. Use a warm, sterilized scoop to pour the jam into the funnel.

JAR LIFTER

Handling the heated jars requires specialized tongs known as jar lifters.

JAM THERMOMETER

This is beneficial for checking the setting point even though it is unnecessary. Pick one with a clip so you can fasten it to the pan's side and a temperature range of at least 230°F.

JELLY BAG

Pre-made jelly bags in a plastic stand that fits over a bowl work best to filter the juices from cooked fruit. However, you may also create your own by tying nylon, muslin, a clean tea towel, or unbleached muslin across the legs of an upright stool.

MUSLIN

You'll need muslin squares to hold stones and spices that must be cooked with jams and chutneys. The components can be wrapped in a sizable square of fabric, then tied into a bag with twine or natural string. Alternatively, you can purchase tiny drawstring muslin bags designed for this use.

SEALING

Hot jam needs to be sealed after being poured into jars. Mason jars have a seal that is a lid component, whereas regular jars need special care. In Britain, we make use of wax disks in a range of sizes. A layer of paraffin wax is favored in the United States and is easily accessible wherever canning ingredients are sold. Make careful to melt the paraffin according to the manufacturer's directions, then pour it.

LABELS

To know how long your preserves have been stored, label everyone. This information must also be marked on chutneys and pickles since they benefit from aging.

PRESERVING TECHNIQUES

There are two fundamental ways to make jam. The traditional approach is boiling the fruit to the set point before adding the sugar. The fruit and sugar must be combined using the macerating process, which calls for ideally overnight soaking to draw out the juices and enhance the taste before boiling to a set. This technique produces a jam that sets more slowly and has a syrupier consistency.

JAM: THE TRADITIONAL METHOD
COOKING THE FRUIT

The amount of water needed will depend on the type of fruit; add the fruit to the preserving pan. Bush fruits may not require water because they quickly break down and release their juices when heated and mashed with a spoon. However, more complex fruits will unquestionably require additional water and a longer boiling time to soften and release the pectin and acid. Gently simmer the fruits. Cooking plums and blueberries until their skins are tender is recommended. Skins may turn tough if sugar is added if cooked through less before.

ADDING THE SUGAR

Use white granulated sugar. The amount of sugar needed varies, but the minimum amount recommended for 1 pound of bulky fruit is 1⅓ cups. Ideally, 1½–1¾ cups for a softer-set jam and 2 cups for a traditionally prepared jam. With experience, you'll discover the effect you prefer.

Before adding the sugar to the fruit, it is preferable to reheat it in a bowl in the oven for about 20 minutes on the lowest setting. This will hasten the sugar's dissolution. To prevent the jam from boiling when the sugar is added, turn off the heat and let the mixture cool slightly. Stirring frequently over low heat will ensure that the sugar dissolves fully. (If the jam boils before the sugar dissolves, it may crystallize while stored.)

BOILING THE JAM

Turn, raise the heat, and boil the jam once the sugar has dissolved. With practice, how long it needs to cook for different things will become more apparent. A high temperature must be maintained for the jam to diminish and thicken, allowing it to set as it cools. Depending on how much water the backup contains, this process can take only a few minutes in some cases and up to 30. Often referred to as a rolling boil, this phase.

TESTING FOR SETTING POINT

The jam should be checked to see if it has reached the setting point after 5 to 10 minutes of fast boiling. There are various ways to do this (see below). While doing the test, turn off the heat to prevent overcooking the jam.

THE COLD PLATE TEST

Place a small plate in the freezer so that it can get cold. Draw your finger through the jam after spooning a small pool onto the plate and letting it cool briefly. It will wrinkle if the setting point has been achieved. Instead of dripping off the plate when you lift your finger off of it, the jam will form a thread.

USING A JAM THERMOMETER

Push the thermometer into the jam, preferably in the middle of the pan, after dipping it in boiling water. The setting point is attained when the temperature reaches 220°F.

THE FLAKE TEST

Hold a wooden spoon above the pan after dipping it into the jam. Allow the spot to drop off the spoon and back into the pan after cooling it briefly. The setting stage is reached when the hole becomes sticky, forming strands or flakes clinging to the spoon.

Place the pan back on the heat and quickly bring it to a boil while testing it every five minutes to see if the setting point has been reached.

SKIMMING

When jam, jelly, or marmalade is boiling, bubbles occasionally rise to the surface and cause scum to form on the surface. Despite being innocuous, this slime can ruin the preserve's look. To assist in spreading the scum, stir in a small glob of butter or scoop it out with a metal spoon.

DISPERSING THE FRUIT

Significant bits of fruit or whole fruits frequently ascend to the top of a jam, where they are likely to remain while the jam sets. If you're creating a softer-set backup with fragments, you might have to put up with it. However, if you want a thicker set, wait 5 to 10 minutes before putting the jam in the jars, and then stir it to spread the pieces evenly.

FILLING AND STORING

Prepare your hot jars and funnel for pots. If using a mason jar, pour the jam into the jar leaving a ¼-inch space between the top of the hole and the rim. If using regular lids with paraffin wax, leave a ½-inch length. Apply paraffin as soon as possible if using. Use mason or other canning jars as the manufacturer directs for covering and sealing. Once the jam has cooled, please keep it in a cold, dry cabinet or pantry.

JAM: THE MACERATING METHOD

Before cooking, letting fruit and sugar macerate together pulls out the fruit's juices and moisture, preserving its flavor. Depending on how sweet the fruit is, cooking times are shortened, flavors are enhanced, and lesser sugar content can be used.

After preparing the fruit as instructed, please place it in a ceramic, glass, or stainless steel bowl. Add the sugar, cover with a plate or press a piece of waxed paper into the fruit's surface to trap the moisture, and allow the fruit to macerate for 6 hours, or up to 3 hours, depending on how complex the fruit is. You'll observe how the sugar absorbs the juices and how a sizable volume of liquid dissolves the sugar.

Once the fruit has been added to a preserving pan, occasionally stir over low heat until all the sugar has dissolved. Sometimes the mixture is allowed to macerate once more, but if not, proceed with heating the jam to the set point and pouring it into the jars.

MAKING MARMALADE

Depending on your method, it can take 1½–3 hours to cook the citrus rind to create citrus marmalade properly. My preferred technique is to poach the oranges whole, but another option is to remove and shred the shell at the beginning. For fruits that have been waxed, you must scrub them first; for fruits that have not been waxed, a simple rinse will do.

POACHING

Place the washed entire fruits in a large, tightly-fitting casserole with a cover. When the fruits float, add just enough water to cover them. Cover the pan and place it in a 350°F preheated oven to poach for 2½–3 hours, by which time the skins will have softened. When the fruit is cold enough to handle, please remove it from the liquid, cut it in half, and scoop out the insides, saving all the seeds and pith and collecting any juice. Make strips of the rind. Put the roots and center in a muslin square, then bundle them with twine. Reintroduce the cooking liquid and any juice that has been gathered.

PARING THE RIND FIRST

Fruits should be cut in half, with the juice squeezed out and collected. Maintain the seeds. Slice the rind into fine strips after paring. Finely chop the pith. Put the roots in a muslin square, then bundle them with thread. Place everything in a pan, cover with water, and soak everything overnight. Bring to a boil the following day, then reduce the heat and simmer for about 1½ hours or until the rind is cooked through. Take away the seed packet.

The procedure is the same moving forward, whatever preparation you use. Warm the sugar before adding, stirring to dissolve, then make jam as usual. If using the poaching method, remove the muslin bag after the marmalade reaches the setting stage and mix to disperse the rind shreds before pouring it into jars.

MAKING JELLIES

While jelly and jam are similar, jelly doesn't have any fruit. Water is used for cooking the fruit, which is then placed into a jelly bag and allowed to drip. The juice alone is utilized. Fruits most suited for creating jelly typically include a lot of pectins.

When creating jellies, first thaw the fruit in water until pliable. The fruit can now be mashed with a spoon before being poured into a jelly bag suspended over a container to capture the drips. Allowing the juice to flow through for an extended period—overnight is ideal—will produce the most transparent jelly. Avoid squeezing the bag, which can obscure the jelly. (It is frequently possible to reboil the jelly bag's contents with half as much water and then pass it through the bag once more to extract the most significant amount of juice and pectin from the fruit.)

Now calculate how much sugar is required by measuring the juice. The general ratio is ¾ cup of sugar to 1 cup of liquid, providing approximately 1 pound and 10 ounces of jelly. Warm the sugar in a preserving pan, then add the juice and whisk to dissolve it entirely. To revert the setting point, bring to a fast boil and cook over high heat as before.

Instead of throwing away the jelly bag residue, pass it through a food processor, collect the purée, and sweeten it for pie filling.

MAKING CURDS

Fruit curds last only two months in a relaxed environment, less time than jams and jellies. Make these in small jars since they must be refrigerated after being opened and consumed within two weeks. Curds can also be poured into suitable containers and frozen for six months.

Because curds are produced with sugar, butter, and eggs, they resemble custard more than jam. They work best with fruity, tangy flavors. It is better to use a double boiler or a basin placed over a pan of simmering water to prevent the eggs from curdling or cooking on high heat. The curd must be continuously stirred for 20 to 30 minutes before it thickens and coats the back of the spoon, but the outcome will be well worth the work.

The first step in making a fruit purée is to cook the fruit until tender with the least amount of water possible. Gooseberries and squash demand more cooking than softer fruits like raspberries and blueberries. Gather the purée after running the fruit through a food mill's fine disk or a sieve.

MAKING CHUTNEYS AND PICKLES

Fruits and vegetables are combined with vinegar, sugar, and spices to make chutneys. They are simple to create; typically, all the ingredients must be integrated and boiled for a few hours in a preserving pan. Packing in jars with vinegar-proof lids is crucial.

Try to wait for 6 to 8 weeks, or even a few months, for chutneys and pickles to mature before consuming them because the tastes get better with time.

All the recipes in this book provide directions for producing the spiced kinds of vinegar needed for pickles and chutneys from scratch. The following recipes, which include two for pickling types of vinegar and two for sweetened pickling vinegar types that may be used to pickle fruits and produce fruit chutneys, also allow you to make your kinds of vinegar.

PICKLING VINEGAR

TO 1 QUART CIDER, MALT, OR WINE VINEGAR, ADD:

- Piece of fresh gingerroot approx. ¾ x 2½ inches, peeled and finely sliced
- 1 tbsp every black peppercorn, mustard seeds, celery seeds
- Eight dried red chilies
- 2 tsp every whole allspice, whole cloves, and whole coriander seeds

Divide the mixture of all the spices among sterile, clean bottles. Add vinegar to the bottles, then cap them with stoppers or corks. Allow the vinegar to steep for 6 to 8 weeks, shaking the bottles occasionally. Before using, remove the spices from the vinegar.

FOR A QUICKER VERSION:

Use a double boiler, throw all the ingredients in a dish, and set it over a pan of simmering water. Spices should steep in the heated vinegar for two to three hours after the vinegar has warmed through without boiling. Before using, remove the herbs from the vinegar.

SWEET PICKLING VINEGAR

TO 1 QUART CIDER, MALT:

- One cinnamon stick
- 1 tbsp every whole allspice, whole coriander seeds, whole cloves, white peppercorns
- Five blades of mace
- Two dried red chilies
- 3½ cups of brown

Divide the mixture of spices into fresh bottles. Fill the bottles with the vinegar and cap them with corks or stoppers after warming the vinegar and dissolving the sugar. Allow the bottles to steep for 6 to 8 weeks while occasionally shaking them. Before using, remove the spices from the vinegar.

FOR A QUICKER VERSION:

Place 2½ cups of white wine vinegar, a rounded ¾ cup of sugar, and a ¾-inch square piece of fresh gingerroot, in a skillet with a few whole allspice berries and black peppercorns, and stir to dissolve the sugar over low heat. Increase the heat, bring it to a boil, and then turn off the heat. Before using, remove the spices from the vinegar.

MAKING NECTARS AND SYRUPS

Fruit that is overripe and unfit for jam-making can be used to make nectars and syrups, which are very simple. The best ingredients are citrus fruits, foraged items like rose hips, elderberries, and elderflowers, and bush fruits like blackberries, loganberries, and raspberries.

The process is the same for all bush fruits. Break up the fruit with a spoon and place it in a bowl. Add very little, if any, water after that. Heat the bowl over a pan of simmering water until the fruit has released all of its juice. Juice from the fruit should drop overnight after being put through a jelly bag to collect.

Add a scant 1½ cups of sugar to every 2 cups of juice and stir together over low heat until dissolved; do not allow it to boil. Fill clean bottles to the 1-inch mark from the top after straining. Use bottles with ceramic stoppers and wires or firmly cork containers. To ensure that the contents of the bottles last for an extended period, they must now be sterilized. (An alternative, and by far the simpler one, is to pour the syrup or nectar into the appropriate containers and freeze them.)

Place the bottles on top of folded newspaper or a trivet in a pan to sterilize them. Fill the bottles almost to the top with cold water, then boil the mixture for 20 minutes.

Once the bottles are properly sealed, store them somewhere cool and dry.

KEEPING TIMES

The other preserves last for six to twelve months, while the jams and jellies are stored unopened in an excellent, dark spot for at least six months. Once jars and bottles are opened, keeping times will vary, but you'll discover that these preserves are so wonderful that they will be consumed long before any possibility of them going bad.

PROBLEM-SOLVING

WHY JAM GOES MOLDY

Mold is most frequently brought on by inadequate sealing of the jam while it is still boiling. As an alternative, jars might have been used that were chilly or damp, not filled, or kept in a wet location. Other potential causes include inadequate water evaporation during the initial heating and insufficient boiling time after the added sugar. Jam with a solid set will last longer than mess with a softer background, which will deteriorate more quickly. Mold may occasionally appear because the fruit was harvested on a muggy day. Decay may change the flavor of the jam, but it won't make it unusable. The backup can be removed, boiled, and placed in brand-new, sanitized jars.

WHY TINY BUBBLES APPEAR

Bubbles are a sign of fermentation, typically when there is not enough sugar relative to the amount of fruit. Jam's sugar content may change if the jam is not reduced enough.

WHY FRUIT RISES IN THE JAM

When fruit is cut up into significant bits or utilized whole, like strawberries, the pieces often rise to the surface of the jam after it has been poured. After the setting point is achieved, stir the spot for 10 to 15 minutes to let it slightly thicken before pouring it into the jars to keep the seeds evenly distributed throughout the preserve. Fruit will always rise because softer-set jams have a syrupy consistency. The same technique of waiting and stirring applies if there is a rind in the marmalade.

WHY JAM CRYSTALLIZES

The usual culprits are too much sugar or not enough acid. The addition of acid in the form of lemon juice enhances low-acid fruits. Before bringing the jam to a rapid boil, ensure the sugar is completely dissolved. Sometimes overripe fruit or overheated storage conditions are to blame.

WHY JAM WON'T SET

Reaching the setting point may be challenging due to low pectin levels brought on by utilizing fruits with low pectin or overripe fruit. Other causes include under-boiling the fruit, which prevents the pectin from being adequately extracted. The jam should be returned to the preserving pan and boiled again. Additionally, the spot can be overcooked when added sugar, a problem for which there is no fix. You can increase the pectin content in fruits like strawberries and cherries with low pectin content.

WHY JAM SHRINKS IN THE JAR

Jam improperly covered, sealed, or not kept in a cool, dark, and dry environment will shrink.

JAMS

Try to jam between the layers of a cake, add a tsp to some vanilla ice cream, or use it to flavor some plain rice pudding. Jam isn't only for spreading on bread. Jam is fruit and sugar cooked together so that the fruit will last longer. You can either puree the fruit or leave it in bits to add texture. One of life's lovely little extras results as a result.

IT MAKES ABOUT 3¾ CUPS

- 4 pints blackberries
- 1-star anise
- Three cloves
- One small cinnamon stick
- juice of 2 lemons
- 3 cups of warmed sugar

- spiced blackberry jam

In general, I love for the simple fruit tastes to predominate while creating jam, but in this case, a combined handful of toasty spices fits this seasonal fruit preserve well.

1. Add the blackberries, star anise, cloves, cinnamon stick, and 2 tbsp of water to a saucepan. This is just enough water to prevent the fruit from sticking to the pan. When they are juicy and tender, mash them with a spoon after bringing them to a simmering temperature.
2. After removing the cinnamon stick, pass the berries through a sieve or a food mill's fine disk. There is no need to purée the fruit at all if you like a chunkier-textured jam; remove the spices with a spoon and stir in the blackberry pulp.
3. Blackberries are placed in a preserving pan with the lemon juice added and heated while gently stirring. Turn raise the heat and quickly boil the jam to every setting point after adding the warmed sugar to the pan and stirring until all of it has dissolved. If required, skim.
4. Transfer the jam to warm, sterile jars.

IT MAKES ABOUT 4¾ CUPS

- 4 pints blackberries
- 1-star anise
- Three cloves
- One small cinnamon stick
- Four nectarines (approx. ½ pound when skinned and stoned)
- juice of 2 lemons
- 4 cups of warmed sugar

SPICED BLACKBERRY & NECTARINE JAM

When I found a cheap pack of nectarines at the store, I came up with this pairing. Along with a pleasing texture, they add an excellent sharpness to the mellow blackberry flavor.

The blackberries and spices should be cooked and puréed as in stages 1-2.

Put the nectarines in a dish and cover them with boiling water to peel them. After a few minutes, drain the water and replenish it with cold water; the fruit's skins should quickly come off. After removing the stones, cut the nectarines into quarters and thirds (smaller pieces if you like a finer-textured preserve). Blackberries, nectarines, sugar, and lemon juice should all be combined in a preserving pan and cooked as in step 3. After 5 minutes, stir the jam to distribute the nectarine chunks evenly. As before, pack the hole.

IT MAKES ABOUT 3¾ CUPS

- 2 pounds apricots
- 3 cups of sugar
- juice of 1 small lemon

APRICOT JAM

The apricots are still in significant bits in this jam, which has a softer set than most since it has less sugar than usual. Since the fruit won't be suspended equally throughout the spot, it will inevitably rise to the top of the jar. This is unimportant; allot one-half of apricot for every serving. For instance, if you want to fill a biscuit, one apricot piece will be cut precisely under the knife. The flavor is maintained at its peak by minimizing cooking time.

- To skin the fruits, put them in a basin, cover them with boiling water, let them sit for a few minutes, and then pour cold water over them. The skins should be simple to remove. The skins should be set aside. Cut the fruit in half and take off the stones. Put the skins and stones inside a piece of muslin, then knot a string bag over it.
- Place the muslin bag with the other ingredients in a ceramic or glass bowl with the sugar, lemon juice, and ¼ cup of water. Place the bowl in the refrigerator for the night and push a wax paper down over the surface to cover it.
- The fruit juice will be extracted and added to the partially dissolved sugar the following day. When the sugar has completely dissolved, pour the bowl's contents into a preserving pan and cook slowly while stirring the mixture. To keep the apricot halves whole, slowly simmer for 10 minutes without going. Then, using a slotted spoon, remove the halves from the syrup. Take out and throw away the muslin bag.
- The syrup should be boiled and quickly reach the set point. Immediately add the apricots back to the syrup and promptly heat to a boil. Jam should be taken off the heat. If required, skim.
- Transfer the apricots to sterilized, hot jars.

- After splitting them equally, drizzle the syrup on top. They did so, filling the jars. The jars should be sealed and left to cool upside-down.

IT MAKES ABOUT 3¾ CUPS

- One vanilla bean
- 2 pounds apricots
- 3 cups of sugar
- juice of 1 small lemon

APRICOT & VANILLA JAM

This combination is very French. This preserve can be enjoyed as a dessert, perhaps with unsweetened whipped cream, because of its softer, syrupier set. Or eat it with a croissant and a cup of coffee.

Cut the vanilla pod in half lengthwise, then use a knife to scrape the seeds. Afterward, prepare apricot jam according to the directions, adding the sources when combining the ingredients in a bowl and hiding the pod pieces among the fruit. Then, let the mixture macerate for an overnight period. The pod fragments must be removed before the jars can be filled and sealed.

IT MAKES ABOUT 3½ CUPS

- 3 pints of white currant
- Four red gooseberries
- juice of 1 lemon
- Two red chilies

WHITE CURRANT & RED CHILI JAM

Another fruit with a great tart flavor and the right consistency for jam-making is white currants. This jam is mild enough to be eaten on sourdough bread for breakfast, thanks to adding chili, and it may also be amplified by adding more chili as needed and using it as a relish to pair with cheese. Additionally, red gooseberries will give this jam a lovely rose color if you mix them with the currants.

1. Use a fork's tines to scrape the white currants' stems clean of their stalks. If using, put the currants, gooseberries, and 5/8 cup of water in a pan, along with the lemon juice. Simmer for a while until the fruit is ripe and bursting.

2. Pass the fruit through a food mill's fine disk or a sieve, gathering the purée that results in a measuring pitcher.
3. For every cup of purée, use ¼ cup of sugar.
4. Add the minced chilies to the purée while still heated, followed by the warmed sugar. Until the sugar has completely dissolved, stir the jam over low heat. Turn the heat up, and boil quickly until the setting point is reached. If required, skim.
5. Fill the heated, sterile jars with the jam.

IT MAKES ABOUT 4 CUPS

- 4 pints raspberries
- juice of 1 small lemon
- 3 cups of warmed sugar

RASPBERRY JAM

Some people enjoy jam with many seeds, whereas others don't. You can choose raspberry jam, for example. For a smoother finish, pass the softened fruit through a sieve if you enjoy the flavor of this fruit but dislike the bothersome seeds. The end product will taste just as excellent as the variety that contains seeds.

1. In a preserving pan, mix the raspberries and lemon juice. Gently warm them to release the juice, then mash the berries with a spoon to soften the fruit and release the liquid. Push the fruit through a sieve to remove the seeds if you want a smooth jam.
2. When the sugar has completely dissolved, add the warmed sugar to the fruit and continue stirring over low heat. Turn to increase the heat and quickly boil the jam until it

IT MAKES ABOUT 5 CUPS

- 1-pint gooseberry stems, and blossom ends removed
- 2 pints strawberries, hulled
- 4 cups of warmed sugar
- juice of 1 lemon

STRAWBERRY & GOOSEBERRY JAM

Gooseberries and strawberries go well together because the higher pectin levels in the former balance the latter's lower levels. I also appreciate jam that looks colorful and tastes delicious; this one succeeds on both counts.

1. Add the gooseberries and 3 tbsp of water to a preserving pan. Add the strawberries after simmering the berries until they are barely tender. Cook for 5 minutes until the fruit wits and the juice runs.
2. Fruit should be combined with hot sugar and lemon juice. Over low heat, stir slowly until the sugar is completely dissolved. Increase the heat and boil the liquid quickly to the set point. If necessary, skim.
3. Fill hot, sterilized jars with the jam and seal them.

IT MAKES ABOUT 4 CUPS

- One vanilla bean
- 4 pints strawberries, hulled; larger fruits halved
- Three scant cups of sugar
- juice of 3 small lemons

STRAWBERRY & VANILLA JAM

Strawberry Jam is undoubtedly the original classic. For the tastiest jam, use this delicate fruit as soon as it is in season and preserve it in easily identifiable chunks. This is a jar of summer. In this recipe, I've paired vanilla with strawberries, the perfect couple you can never have enough of.

If you're feeling gluttonous, you may eat this strawberry jam straight from the jar because it has a softer set and contains a little less sugar than the typical strawberry jam. Mix a few spoonfuls of it for a quick dessert with plain yogurt and mascarpone. Alternatively, spoon it onto a hot biscuit and eat it immediately before the jam runs out the sides.

1. Cut the vanilla bean in half lengthwise, then arrange the strawberry and vanilla bean pieces in a basin. Leave the sugar-covered surface for 12 or even 24 hours.
2. In a preserving pan, add the lemon juice after adding the fruit, vanilla bean, and juice. Cook the fruit without stirring for the cooking process over low heat until

the sugar has completely dissolved. Heat the liquid and boil it quickly to the set point. If required, skim.
3. Take the vanilla bean pieces out and scrape the seeds out. Add the roots to the jam and discard the bean bits. The origins and spot should be combined.
4. Fill hot, sterilized jars with the jam, then seal them.

IT MAKES ABOUT 2½ CUPS

- 1 pound plums, halved and stoned

PLUM JAM

The Blaisdon Red plum is my favorite for this jam because it is a locally cultivated plum variety where I reside. There is always a lot of spot-making because, in most years, the trees are dripping with them towards the end of the summer. Other plum cultivars will undoubtedly perform just as well.

1. The plums should be tender but intact after 10 minutes of gentle cooking when placed in a pan with ½ cup of water.
2. When all the sugar has dissolved, add the warmed sugar to the fruit and stir over low heat. Then, increase the heat and boil the mixture to achieve the set point. If required, skim.
3. Jam should be added to a heated, sterile

DAMSON JAM

One of the tastiest jams is made with damsons. It is a traditional fruit that isn't typically utilized in commercial preserves. This fruit is perfect for a single-fruit jam because of its assertive and conventional characteristics.

Use damsons in the Plum Jam recipe; do not try to remove the stones before cooking. Once the cooked fruit has cooled, use your hands to find and remove the remaining stones after scooping off any that float to the top. Add the sugar and reheat to the setting point as usual once all the rocks have been removed.

IT MAKES ABOUT 5 CUPS

- 1 pound plums, halved and stoned
- 1 pound marrow squash flesh, cut into chunks
- 4 cups of sugar

PLUM & MARROW SQUASH JAM

Just a few plums can go a long way with the help of a fantastic jam. In this recipe, the marrow squash transforms into a chameleon, thickening the jam and soaking up the delicious sweetness of the plums.

Mix the plums and marrow squash in a skillet with ½ cup of water as in Plum Jam.

IT MAKES ABOUT 5 CUPS

- 3 pints raspberries
- 1½ pounds ripe peaches
- 4¼ cups of sugar
- juice of 2 lemons

EVERY & RASPBERRY JAM

This jam's rich red raspberries and scattered bits give it a magnificently vibrant appearance and fabulous fragrance. As usual, I would choose a chunky texture, in this case, to distinguish this preserve from anything you might ever buy in a store. Of course, you may chop the peaches more finely.

1. Raspberries should be put in a pan. Mash them with a spoon to soften and release their juice after gentle warming.
2. Push them through a sieve or the fine disk of a food grinder when they are soft and juicy.
3. Mix the raspberry purée, half the sugar, and half the lemon juice in a saucepan. Simmer for a few minutes, then remove from the heat and transfer to a glass or ceramic bowl. Put the waxed paper on top, pressing it firmly onto the fruit, and place the bowl in the refrigerator for the night.
4. In the meantime, put the peaches in a basin and cover them with boiling water to skin them. After a few minutes of steeping, the skins should now easily peel away from the flesh. Drain the water and replenish it with cold water. To ensure the pieces are still reasonably large, quarter the peaches, remove the stones, and cut every quarter in half.
5. Mix the peaches, remaining sugar, and lemon juice in a skillet. Heat the mixture until it simulates, then turns off the heat. As with the raspberries, place the fruit in a glass or ceramic bowl and wrap it in waxed paper before placing it in the refrigerator for the night.

6. The following day, put the peaches and raspberries in a saucepan and gently boil while constantly stirring to ensure the sugar has completely dissolved.
7. Increase the heat and boil the mixture until the setting point is reached. If required, skim. Stir to spread every bit after 5 minutes. Fill hot, sterilized jars with the jam, then seal them.

IT MAKES ABOUT 3 CUPS

- 2 pints cherries
- One generous cup of warmed sugar
- 1 tbsp lemon juice

CHERRY JAM

For this jam, you can either use a dark cooking cherry, such as a Morello cherry, or a lighter dessert cherry; the color of your spot will change correspondingly. If you cultivate your own, harvest them as soon as they are mature; otherwise, the birds will consume them all before you can.

1. Pit the cherries over a basin to capture juice using a cherry stoner. Put the stones in a muslin bag with a string bag knotted over it. The fruit and fluid should be placed in a skillet with 2 tbsp of water and gently simmered until barely tender.
2. Stir the fruit with the warmed sugar and lemon juice over low heat until all the sugar has dissolved. Increase the heat and immediately bring the mixture to a boil to reach the set point. After removing the muslin bag, swirl the jam to evenly distribute the cherries before allowing it to rest for 5 to 10 minutes. Skim if required.
3. The spot must be placed into warm, sterilized jars before being sealed.

IT MAKES ABOUT 8 CUPS

- 2¼ cups of rose hips
- 2¼ cups of hawthorn hips ("haws")
- 2 cups of rowan berries
- 2 cups of sloes
- 1 pound crab apples
- 2 pints blackberries
- 1½ pints elderberries

- ⅞ cup of hazelnuts, shelled and chopped
- warmed sugar; for quantity

COUNTRYSIDE JAM

Gathering food for nothing that has required zero effort to develop is such a fulfilling activity. I made this jam using a combination of fruits purchased in any reputable supermarket and the numerous tasty fruits England's hedgerows produce in the fall. Although rowan (European mountain ash) does not typically grow wild in the United States, any area with woodlands or farmland will have valuable ingredients. You must adopt a flexible strategy because only some of your selected fruits will be ripe simultaneously. Because only some berries are edible, this jam is only for you if you know how to identify the ones. Autumn in a Jar is Countryside Jam.

1. Sort the fruit and take the stalks out. Put the apples, sloes, hips, haws, and, if using, rowan berries in a pan with just enough water to cover the fruit, causing it to start floating. Fifteen minutes should be plenty for the fruit to soften and the apples to become fluffy.
2. Pull the puréed pulp from the fruit mixture in a preserving pan, passing it through a food mill's fine disk or a sieve. Fifteen minutes later, add the nuts, elderberries, and blackberries.
3. Add the same amount of hot sugar after measuring the cooked fruit. Once all the sugar has completely dissolved, stir over low heat, then increase the heat and boil quickly to the set point. if required, skim
4. Fill hot, sterilized jars with the jam, then seal them.

IT MAKES ABOUT 4 CUPS

- 2 pounds of pears, peeled, cored, and cut into chunky slices
- juice of 1 large lemon
- 3 cups of sugar
- One vanilla bean

PEAR & VANILLA JAM

Another one of my faves that I find difficult to live without is this jam. The pale jam's quality can be seen in the natural vanilla flecks scattered throughout, which give it its fragrant flavor. In this case, macerating the pears also enhances their flavor.

1. Mix the lemon juice with the pears in a basin to prevent them from turning brown. Add ¼ cup of water after sprinkling the sugar over the fruit.
2. Once the vanilla bean's seeds have been removed, cut it in half lengthwise, insert the bean between the pears, and then add the seeds. Overnight, leave the dish covered with a plate so that the fruit juices can soak up some of the sugar.
3. The following day, transfer the bowl's contents into a preserving pan, stir over low heat to dissolve the sugar, then increase the heat and quickly boil until the mixture reaches the setting point, where the pears will be transparent. if required, skim
4. Pour the jam into hot, sterilized jars and seal after removing the vanilla bean.

IT MAKES ABOUT 4 CUPS

- 1 pound apricots
- Four stalks (approx. 1 pound) of rhubarb, cut into short lengths
- 3 cups of sugar
- juice of 1 lemon

RHUBARB & APRICOT JAM

This jam is undoubtedly a superstar. Everyone who has tried it has been blown away by how flavorful it is and how perfectly this blend of fruits works together. It's also a wonderful treat visually because of the big apricot halves and the pink hue of the rhubarb chunks. This is the jam to make if you only make one in the book (although, hopefully, you'll make more than that!).

1. By putting the apricots in a bowl and covering them with boiling water, you can skin them. After waiting a short while, drain the water and replace it with cold water. With a knife, the skins should then be simple to remove. Remove the stones before cutting them into halves.
2. After mixing everything, cover the bowl with a plate and let it sit for an hour.
3. When the sugar has completely dissolved, pour the bowl's contents into a preserving pan and stir gently over low heat. Increase the heat, bring it to a simmer, and then turn it off. Everything should be poured into a glass or ceramic bowl, covered with wax paper inserted into the surface, and chilled for the night.

4. The following day, pour the bowl's contents back into the preserving pan, stirring until all the sugar has dissolved. Then, increase the heat and quickly boil until the setting point, skimming as required.
5. Fill hot, sterilized jars with the jam, then seal them.

IT MAKES ABOUT 4½ CUPS.

- Eight stalks (approx. 2¼ pounds) of rhubarb, cut into short lengths
- , finely grated zest, and juice of 3 limes
- 3¾ cups of sugar

RHUBARB & LIME JAM

Rhubarb is frequently paired with orange, but I prefer doing so instead. This medley was created in heaven.

All the ingredients should be combined in a basin, covered with a plate, and left for an hour. Then complete Rhubarb & Apricot Jam steps 3 through 5.

IT MAKES ABOUT 2½ CUPS

- 1 pound figs, stalks removed and chopped into small pieces
- 2 cups of warmed sugar
- juice of 1 lemon

GREEN FIG JAM

Making jam using figs that are green or purple is OK. Pick or purchase figs already ripe enough to use since they do not continue to mature after being plucked from the tree and do not have much flavor when unripe. This jam is seed-studded throughout and has a gorgeous, rich color.

1. The figs should be cooked in a skillet with 2 tbsp of water until tender and juicy.
2. Stir the fruit with the warmed sugar and lemon juice over low heat until the sugar completely dissolves. Then, increase the heat and quickly bring the mixture to a boil to achieve the set point. After 10 minutes, whisk the mixture to distribute the fig chunks evenly. if required, skim
3. Fill hot, sterilized jars with the jam, then seal them.

IT MAKES ABOUT 4½ CUPS

- 1¼ pounds figs
- 1 pound of pears, peeled, cored, and diced
- finely grated zest and juice of 1 large orange and one small lemon
- 3¾ cups of sugar
- Eight green cardamom pods, crushed and pods discarded

FIG & PEAR JAM

Because the two major components in this recipe are poor in pectin, the additions of lemon and orange must help to increase their setting power. Green cardamom seeds give the flavor a distinctive and exciting edge.

After preparing the figs as directed above, mix all the ingredients in a bowl and let sit for an hour. Pour the mixture into a preserving pan, stir to dissolve the sugar, then raise the heat to a simmering temperature. Pour the mixture into a glass or ceramic dish, cover the top with waxed paper, and put the bowl in the refrigerator overnight. Add the ingredients to the pan the next day and stir over low heat. Then, crank the heat and quickly boil until the mixture reaches The setting point. Pack the mixture as before.

IT MAKES ABOUT 2 CUPS

- juice and finely pared zest of 1 small lemon
- 1 pound green tomatoes, finely chopped
- 1⅝ cups of sugar
- Two pieces of stem ginger, about 1 inch in diameter, finely sliced

GREEN TOMATO JAM

Green tomatoes, typically considered a chutney component, were initially widely used to make jam but have since lost their appeal. This recipe will demonstrate the need for a renaissance in fashion. Here, the ginger stem and lemon peel mix to make a candied jam with a stunning hue.

1. Cover the lemon zest with water in a skillet and simmer for about an hour or until tender. Discard the liquid after draining the zest.
2. Mix the tomatoes, lemon juice, and sugar in a bowl to allow the sugar to absorb part of the fruit liquids. Leave the mixture overnight.

3. The following day, transfer the bowl's contents to a preserving pan and include the zest. Once the sugar has completely dissolved, stir over low heat, increase the heat, and quickly boil the mixture to the set point. If required, skim.
4. Pour the jam into hot, sterilized jars and seal after stirring the stem ginger.

GREEN TOMATO & ANGELICA JAM

This combination was mentioned in the 1938 book Tomatoes and How to Grow Them by F. R. Castle. An intriguing herb, angelica grows into a tall, spectacular plant to fit in the perennial border. If fresh angelica is not available, you can find candied stems.

Use two or three fresh stems about 5 inches tall or a scant ¼ cup of candied bits, then make the green tomato jam as directed, but without the stem ginger. Pick young stems of angelica if using fresh. They should be covered with boiling water and let 5 minutes to steep before being drained and finely shredded. First, add to the tomatoes. Instead of using stem ginger, add the candied stems at the end of the process after being finely chopped.

IT MAKES ABOUT 5¼ CUPS

- 1½ cups of black currants
- 1½ cups of red currants
- 2 cups of strawberries
- 2 cups of raspberries
- 4¼ cups of warmed sugar

TUTTI FRUTTI JAM

Small amounts of fruit can be used to make mixed-fruit jams. Use only red currants if you can't locate black ones (not to be confused with little raisins). Combining fruits with high and low pectin content is an intelligent approach to aid the jam's setting.

1. Run the tines of a fork over the stems of the black and red currants to separate them from their stalks. Add the currants and just enough water to prevent the fruits from sticking to the pan's bottom in a preserving pan. After bringing to a boil, simmer for 15 to 20 minutes.
2. For an additional 10 minutes, add the strawberries and raspberries to the pot. When all the sugar has dissolved, add the warmed sugar to the fruit and

continue stirring over low heat. Turn the heat up, and boil quickly until the setting point is reached. If required, skim
3. Fill hot, sterilized jars with the jam, then seal them.

IT MAKES ABOUT 3¾ CUPS

- 2 pints of gooseberries, stems, and blossom ends removed
- Three rounded cups of sugar
- juice of 2 small lemons

GOOSEBERRY JAM

Gooseberries provide a tart jam that goes well with both sweet and savory dishes. The first types, available for picking in the early summer, signal the start of a season filled with delectable fruits. Their acidity makes them perfect for jam-making. Later kinds get sweeter and are suitable for eating raw.

1. In a preserving pan, mix all the ingredients and heat slowly until simmering. Remove the heat immediately, then pour the contents into a glass or ceramic bowl. The waxed paper should be spread over the area and pressed onto the fruit. Place the bowl in the fridge for the night.
2. The following day, re-add the bowl's contents to the preserving pan, boil slowly, and stir to ensure all the sugar has dissolved. Then increase the heat and quickly boil until the setting point is reached. Only 5 to 10 minutes are needed to complete this, and you must watch to ensure the syrup doesn't burn. if required, skim
3. Fill hot, sterilized jars with the jam, then seal them.

IT MAKES ABOUT 3¾ CUPS

- A handful of fresh elderflowers
- 2 pints of gooseberries, stems, and blossom ends removed
- Three rounded cups of sugar
- juice of 2 small lemons

GOOSEBERRY & ELDERFLOWER JAM

How fortunate that elderflowers and early gooseberries are both in season simultaneously. Once more, elderflowers enhance a traditional British dish with their distinct and delicate flavor.

Before wrapping the flowers in muslin and tying them into a bundle, shake the buds face down to eliminate pests. Make gooseberry jam according to the instructions, adding the elderflower bundle after the first boil before letting the gooseberries macerate for the night. Remove the bundle before adding the fruit back to the canning pan for the last cooking period.

IT MAKES ABOUT 4 CUPS

- 1 pound peaches, quartered and stoned
- 1 pound of pears, quartered
- juice of 1 lemon
- 3⅓ cups of sugar

EVERY & PEAR JAM

Another lovely fusion of delicate flavors can be found here. I processed the fruit using a food mill here since I prefer the texture. It provides the jam and requires less initial preparation. If you'd choose, you may leave the fruits whole, but you'll need to peel, core the pears and skin, and stone the peaches beforehand.

1. To release the juices and soften the fruit, place it in a skillet with lemon juice and 1 tbsp water. After ten minutes of simmering, turn off the heat and let the dish cool.
2. To purée the fruit mixture, run it through a food mill's fine disk or a sieve, then transfer the pulp to a preserving pan. When the sugar has completely dissolved, add it to the fruit and stir it over low heat. Increase the heat and quickly bring the mixture to a boil to achieve the set point. if required, skim
3. Fill hot, sterilized jars with the jam, then seal them.

IT MAKES ABOUT 6 CUPS

- 1 pound cooking apples, roughly chopped
- 1 pound of pears, roughly chopped
- 1 pound plums, halved
- 1¼ cup of water
- grated zest and juice of 1 small lemon
- piece of gingerroot, approx. ¾ × 2½ inches, bruised
- Two cloves
- 5 cups of sugar

DUMPSIDEARY JAM

Dumpsideary jam has a charming name that sounds old-fashioned and contains a decadent combination of orchard fruits—apples, pears, and plums—all in season simultaneously. It is sometimes referred to as High Dumpsideary and is lightly spiced with ginger and cloves; sixty is the name of a similar jam without spices. Giving someone a jar of this jam will surely spark conversation just because of the word.

1. Add all the fruits and the plum stones to a preserving pan with 1¼ cups of water, and boil slowly until the fruit is tender.
2. After removing the plum stones, pass the fruit through a food mill's fine disk or a sieve.
3. Put the finished fruit purée, lemon juice, and zest in a preserving pan. Put the sugar and the spices in the pan after tying the herbs in a muslin cloth. Stirring frequently, gradually heat the liquid until all the sugar has dissolved. Turn the heat up, and boil quickly until the setting point is reached. If required, skim.
4. Take the spices out. Put the jam in hot, sterilized jars, then tighten the lids.

JELLIES

Jellies have an appealing clarity and purity since they are made from the fruit juices that have been extracted. When you hold the jar up to the light, it is like looking through stained glass. The amber hues of crab apple, the rich scarlet tints of raspberry and red currant, and the dense darkness of blackberry jellies are tempting.

FOR QUANTITY,

- 2 pounds of black currant
- juice of 1 small lemon (optional)
- warmed sugar, for quantity
- black currant jelly

This jelly has a nicely balanced, rich, tart flavor and is deep black and glassy in appearance. Black currants (Ribes nigrum) are perfect for jams and jellies because of their distinct and robust flavor. They have a long European history and are slowly gaining popularity here, but you could have difficulty getting them. You might think about producing your own (check that your state permits this; for many years, they were banned in some states for ecological reasons).

1. Run a fork through the stems of the black currants to separate them from their stalks.
2. The currants should be simmered for 5 minutes until they begin to burst and the juice flows, in a preserving pan with the lemon juice, if used, and 2 cups of water. Take the pan off the heat, then use a fork to mash the currants.
3. Fill a jelly bag over a bowl with the currants and liquid, and let it drip for several hours or overnight (resisting the urge to help things along by squeezing the bag).
4. Due to the high pectin content of black currants, you can improve the yield by adding the pulp and ¼ cup of water to the preserving pan and boiling it for 5 minutes. Refill the jelly bag with the pulp, drain it for a few hours, and then collect the juice in a pitcher.
5. For every cup of juice, use ¼ cup of sugar.
6. After heating the juice in a preserving pan over low heat, add the warmed sugar. Stir to dissolve the sugar, then increase the heat and quickly boil the mixture to the set point.
7. If required, skim Seal after pouring into hot, sterilized jars.

RED CURRANT & GOOSEBERRY JELLY

You should expect this jelly to have a nice set because red currants and gooseberries are practically tied for first place regarding pectin content. The red currants contribute to the attractive color of the jelly, which the gooseberries cannot provide on their own.

Follow the recipe for Black Currant Jelly, but use 2½ cups of every red currant, gooseberries, and 1½ cups of water. Boil the currants and berries together until soft and bursting, then pour into a jelly bag and collect the juice in a pitcher. Don't boil the fruit pulp a second time. Complete the jelly as before.

FOR QUANTITY,

- 4 cups of rose hips, stalks removed
- 2 pounds cooking or tart apples, roughly chopped
- warmed sugar

ROSE HIP JELLY

Perhaps surprisingly, the juice made from these wild berries has a great flavor and is high in vitamin C. First, drain the hip juice because these fruits are packed with tiny seeds and stinging hairs that are utterly inedible. Because all the undesirable pulp is removed when heating rose hips first and running them through a jelly bag, they are exceptionally well suited for creating jelly.

1. In a preserving pan, mix the apples and rose hips. Simmer them for about 45 minutes, or until the fruit is soft and pulpy, with just enough water to cover them. The fruit should be mashed with the back of a spoon, then poured into a jelly bag, left undisturbed for an entire night, and the drips should be collected in a measuring pitcher.
2. For every cup of juice, add ¼ cup of sugar. Put the juice and warmed sugar in a preserving pan and stir over low heat until the sugar has completely dissolved. Then, increase the heat and boil the mixture to achieve the set point. If required, skim.
3. Seal the jelly after pouring it into hot, sterilized jars.

ROWAN JELLY

From the European mountain ash (Sorbus aucuparia), rowan berries make a jelly that sets well. It is perfect for serving with the game because the apples or quinces balance their slightly bitter flavor.

Mix equal parts of apples and rowan berries for this jelly or quinces if you have any on hand. It is prepared in the same manner as rose hip jelly. However, it tends to sink to the bottom of the jars. Adding chopped rosemary to the jelly before packing works well because this preserve is frequently served with fatty meats.

FOR QUANTITY,

- 2 pounds crab apples, roughly chopped
- sugar

CRAB APPLE JELLY

Although they appear to be a forgotten fruit, crab apples are frequently in plentiful supply in season. Since they are too little to be easily peeled and cored, you can create jelly or purée the fruit to make curds, kinds of butter, or pie fillings. The goal while producing jelly is to have something as transparent as possible.

Jellies made from different apples will have hues ranging from amber to rose, and they always appear stunning when illuminated. Add a few cloves, cinnamon sticks, or gingerroot slices to the fruit before cooking for a spicier variation. But I much instead let the fruit's distinct flavor come through.

1. In a preserving pan with 2 cups of water, add the apples. The fruits should be simmered for around 45 minutes, being mashed with a wooden spoon until they soften and become fluffy.
2. Place the apples in a jelly bag hanging over a measuring pitcher to catch the drips. If you want your jelly crystal clear, resist the urge to crush the bag and let the apples drain naturally for many hours or overnight.
3. Remove the pulp from the bag, put it in a skillet with ¼ cup of water, and bring it back to a boil to release more juice. Please put it back in the bag and let it drain for a few more hours.
4. For every cup of juice, use ¼ cup of sugar. When the sugar is added to the fluid, stir continuously over low heat until all of the sugar has dissolved. Increase the heat and boil the liquid quickly to the set point.
5. If required, skim. Seal the jelly after pouring it into hot, sterilized jars.

FOR QUANTITY,

- 1 pound apples
- 1 pound damsons
- sugar

DAMSON & APPLE JELLY

One of the most troublesome features of damsons is "stoning the fruit," and making the fruit into a jelly is the ideal solution. Leave the job to the jelly bag.

When making crab apple jelly, boil the apples in 2 cups water for 15 minutes before adding the damsons. Fill the jelly bag as usual after adding the mixed fruits.

FOR QUANTITY,

- 1 pound apples
- 1 pound sloes

- sugar

SLOE & APPLE JELLY

Sloes give apple jelly a gorgeous rose hue and a delightfully tangy flavor. This adaptable preserve goes well with savory and sweet foods and may be served with cheeses and meats. The most significant time to harvest sloes is just after the first frost.

As directed in the recipe for Crab Apple Jelly, simmer the apples in 2 cups of water for the first 15 minutes before adding the sloes. Fill a jelly bag with everything and proceed as usual.

FOR QUANTITY,

- 5 pints blackberries
- juice of ½ small lemon
- sugar

BLACKBERRY JELLY

Put kids to work gathering blackberries for this jelly as they enjoy doing so. Blackberry jelly frequently contains spices, but I prefer the actual fruit's flavor to take center stage. Here, I've chosen to use only blackberries and a tiny bit of lemon to help the jelly set.

1. Put the berries and a scant ½ cup of water in a preserving pan. Melt the fruit in a saucepan for 5 minutes, then mash the berries with a wooden spoon.
2. Fruit should be placed in a jelly bag overnight or until the pulp is almost dry. The jelly bag should be suspended over a measuring pitcher to catch drips.
3. For every cup of juice, use ¼ cup of sugar. Blackberry juice is combined with lemon juice before being poured into a preserving pan. Add it and stir over low heat when the sugar is all dissolved. Increase the heat and boil the mixture quickly to revert to the set point.
4. If required, skim. Seal the jelly after pouring it into hot, sterilized jars.

RASPBERRY JELLY

This jelly's gorgeous, jewel-like hue and great fruitiness make it the perfect choice when used as the filling in a layer cake. Also appropriate for those who enjoy raspberries but detest their seeds.

Replace the blackberries with raspberries and proceed as directed for the blackberry jelly.

MARMALADES

" marmalade " typically refers to a citrus fruit preserve eaten with toast for breakfast. Traditional citrus marmalade is best made using bitter Seville oranges. But unlike France, where marmalade is created from different puréed fruits, the first marmalade was made in Portugal using quinces.

IT MAKES ABOUT 4 CUPS

- 1½ pints black currants
- 1 pound of apples, cut into large chunks
- warmed sugar

APPLE & BLACK CURRANT MARMALADE

Black currants give this marmalade precisely the proper amount of sharpness and punch, even though it doesn't contain any citrus fruits, making it ideal for serving breakfast. There is no need to peel or core the apples at the beginning because the food mill separates them from the flesh to produce a purée with some texture. Processing the fruits through a food mill makes the most effective use of the fruit with very little preparation.

The abundance of apples in season is another excellent method to utilize an apple surplus. Since this dish doesn't require perfect specimens, windfalls will work fine.

1. Run the tines of a fork over the stems of the black currants to separate them from their stalks.
2. Add 3 tbsp of water to a pan with all the fruit (just enough to keep the fruit from catching on the bottom). Gently simmer the mixture until the apples are fluffy, the fruit is tender, and the juices flow. Please turn off the heat and let it stand until it is safe to handle.

3. The fruit combination should be forced through a sieve or the fine disk of a food mill into a bowl. Add the same amount of hot sugar after measuring the purée in a preserving pan. Turn to raise the heat and boil quickly to achieve the set point after stirring over low heat until all the sugar has dissolved. If necessary, skim.

4. Put the jam in hot, sterilized jars, then tighten the lids.

APPLE & CRANBERRY MARMALADE

This modification to the previous recipe demonstrates the apples' exceptional adaptability and how they may mix with nearly any fruit. With the help of this template, you may incorporate any fruits you have a sur+ of, using apples as a base, cook and puree them, and then adjust the amount of sugar. Use crab apples or any cooking apple with a solid flavor to make this marmalade, and balance them with another tart fruit.

Use cranberries instead of the black currants in the apple and black currant marmalade recipe.

IT MAKES ABOUT 6 CUPS

- 2 pounds Seville oranges
- One small lemon
- 6 cups of sugar

SEVILLE ORANGE MARMALADE

Seville oranges are only accessible briefly in late winter, but the search for them is worthwhile since they create the best marmalade. They are only used for cooking because of their exceedingly bitter flavor, but when prepared and sweetened, they are incredibly delicious due to their robust nature. You prefer sliced rind or smooth marmalade, but I'll take the nicely cooked, sweetened rind slivers suspended in this amber liquid any day.

1. Preheat the oven to 350 degrees Fahrenheit. Put the whole fruits in an oven-safe, heavy casserole with a lid or preserving pan. Add 5 cups of water to the stovetop and bring it to a simmering point.
2. Place the pan in the oven with a lid made of aluminum foil if you're using a preserving pan. The fruit should be poached for 2½–3 hours to soften the skins.

3. Lift the fruit from the liquid with a spoon and place it in a colander. Cut every fruit in half when cold enough to handle, remove the pulp with a spoon while leaving the skin on, and place the pulp, pith, and seeds in a muslin bag hung over a bowl to catch any drips. (A massive piece of muslin collected into a bag and knotted with string can also be used.) To make the liquid 1 quart in volume, add any that has accumulated in the basin underneath the pulp that has been drained before measuring the liquid.
4. Put the muslin bag in a pot and cover it with enough poaching liquid. Then, simmer for 15 minutes after bringing it to a boil. Squeeze the bag to extract as much juice as you can from the pulp after letting it cool enough to handle. Throw away the bag and everything within.
5. Put the rind in a preserving pan after chopping it into thin pieces. Ultimately add the poaching liquid. You can add the sugar without warming it if the mixture is cold; otherwise, you must heat it first. After the sugar has been well dissolved and the orange liquid is clear, boil it for 15 minutes and test it for a set point.
6. After removing the marmalade from the heat, swirl it to evenly spread the peel and let it stand for 15 minutes. If required, skim Seal after pouring into hot, sterilized jars.

IT MAKES ABOUT 5 CUPS

- 1 pound dried figs
- Three lemons
- 4¾ cups of warmed sugar

LEMON & FIG MARMALADE

It would be wise to experiment with this uncommon pairing. The lemon half-moons are kept whole, giving the preserve a delightful candied flavor. They are a delicious way to start the day, along with the figs.

1. Cut every one of the figs into four pieces after removing the stalks. Lemons should be cut in half lengthwise, then thinly sliced, with the liquid and any seeds collected as you go. Put the roots in a muslin piece, then tie a string bag around it. Mix the figs, the wrapped seeds, lemon slices, and juice in a big dish. Cover with 1 quart of water and let sit for 24 hours.

2. The mixture should simmer for 1–1½ or until the lemon rind is tender after being poured into a skillet and heated to a simmer. Remove the seeds after letting the area cool slightly.
3. Place the warmed sugar in. Bring the marmalade to a fast boil and cook until it reaches the setting point by stirring over low heat without boiling until the sugar has completely dissolved. If required, skim Seal hot, sterilized jars with the pot.

IT MAKES ABOUT 3¼ CUPS

- juice and pared rind of 12 limes
- 3 cups of warmed sugar

LIME MARMALADE

Try this recipe to branch out from the usual orange jam. Here is another practical marmalade you can make any time of the year with the fruit you buy at the supermarket. Excellent in both color and flavor.

Finely shred the rind fragments. Lime seeds and piths should be placed in a muslin bag and secured with string. Mix the lime rind, juice, and 7 cups of water in a preserving pan. Bring to a boil, then simmer to soften the shell for an hour. Add the warmed sugar and whisk over low heat when all the sugar has completely dissolved. Next, increase the heat and boil the mixture to achieve the set point. Pour the marmalade into warm, sterilized jars, then remove the muslin bag before sealing.

IT MAKES ABOUT 4 CUPS

- 2 pounds of peaches, roughly chopped
- 3¼ cups of sugar

EVERY MARMALADE

My go-to breakfast spread is often a tart citrus preserve, but this fragrant, a little softer marmalade makes for a great start to the day. Of course, you may have it whenever you want, but my favorite time to eat it is in the morning. The fruit's wonderful perfume is enhanced by cooking, and the variation below, which includes vanilla, results in an even more luxurious sensation.

1. Mix the peaches with their stones and 1 cup of water in a pan. They should be simmered for a while until every bit is tender.
2. Throw away the stones and purée the meat by pressing it through a sieve or the fine disk of a food mill.
3. Mix the purée with the sugar in a preserving pan, warming it if required, and gently stir until it is entirely dissolved. Boil at a higher temperature until the liquid reaches the setting point. If necessary, skim.
4. Put the jam in hot, sterilized jars, then tighten the lids.

EVERY & VANILLA MARMALADE

This breakfast favorite gets an undeniable taste boost from vanilla. Peaches already have a beautiful aroma, so when vanilla is added, they become just divine. The vanilla bean's scraped seeds, which are sticky black, are scattered throughout the jam. It goes great on toast for breakfast and makes a superb sweet treat any time of day.

When cooking the peaches with the above water, split a vanilla bean lengthwise and add it to the fruit. Before puréeing the fruit, remove the bean and, using a sharp knife, scrape the seeds from the bean pieces. Bean fragments are discarded after stirring the roots into the very purée. Proceed as before.

IT MAKES ABOUT 4¼ CUPS

- 2 pounds quinces, fur washed off
- Three small oranges
- warmed sugar

QUINCE & ORANGE MARMALADE

According to legend, the first marmalade was a quince preserve, hence the name Carmelo, which is Portuguese for this fruit. Quince is a forgotten fruit that is rarely sold. However, you might find it in Mediterranean grocery stores. If you have a quince tree, you can make a fantastic marmalade by combining these beautiful fruits with oranges. They are cooked at a shallow temperature to enhance the flavor and bring out the best in the quinces; for a similar outcome, cook the marmalade in a slow cooker.

1. Use a second casserole if all the fruits won't fit into the first one. Place the fruits in the dish and fill them with boiling water until they barely start to float. Put

the lid on and cook slowly for 6 to 8 hours in the oven, overnight, or in a slow cooker.
2. When it is safe to handle, take the baking sheet out of the oven. Colander the liquid and pour it into a pan. Place the quinces' skins and cores with the cooking liquid after quartering and peeling them. Scoop out the meat from 2 of the oranges, cut them in half, and add the flesh, seeds, and pith to the liquid. Place the peel aside.
3. Bring the mixture to a boil before reducing it to a third or a half of its initial volume. Through a strainer, pour the thickened mixture into a preserving pan.
4. Slice the quinces into thick slices that measure ½ inches and ¾ inches in diameter. Slice the entire orange into thin rounds, then finely shred the removed orange halves.
5. Once the mixture has been reduced, add the quinces, orange slices, and shredded rind and heat through. Keeping the orange slices whole, add the same volume of warmed sugar and whisk over low heat until all the sugar has dissolved. Then, increase the heat and boil quickly to achieve the set point. If required, skim.
6. With the help of a slotted spoon, remove the orange slices and use them to decorate the heated, sterilized jars' interiors by leaning them against the glass. Then, tightly cap the jars with the marmalade.

FRUITS IN SYRUP

Fruits and vegetables were typically preserved by bottling them in water or sugar syrup before the invention of the freezer. Fruits in syrup have a far more opulent feel now that bottling is a specialized activity and freezing is the standard. They are excellent gifts when placed in attractive jars and spiced or flavored.

IT MAKES ABOUT 1½ PINTS

- 1¾ cups of sugar
- pared rind and juice of 1 small orange
- One small cinnamon stick
- Four cardamom pods, with seeds crushed
- 2-star anise
- 1½ pounds apricots, halved and stoned

APRICOTS IN SYRUP

If you come across any delicious apricots, this is an excellent way to use them. This bottled fruit is exceptionally special—special enough to offer by itself as dessert after a meal—thanks in large part to the syrup, which is quite peppery. It also looks nice if the spices are still intact in the container.

1. Create a syrup by combining 2½ cups of water, sugar, three strips of orange zest, juice, and spices in a pan. Before increasing the heat and bringing the mixture to a simmer, heat it slowly to dissolve the sugar.
2. The apricots should be added and poached until cooked in whole pieces. Then, using a slotted spoon, remove the apricots and pack them into hot, sterilized jars. To thicken and decrease the syrup, rapidly bring it to a boil for 10–15 minutes.
3. Cover the fruit thoroughly with the syrup and spices. Seal the jars after giving them a little tap to remove any air bubbles.

NECTARINES IN SYRUP

Nectarines, one of the summer's most delicious fruits, are also a wonderful delight when preserved, ready for an "encore" in the fall or winter.

Nectarines can be used in place of the apricots in Apricots in Syrup in the same amount. With the stones removed, medium-sized fruits can be sliced in half, while bigger fruits should be quartered. as you would for the main recipe.

DAMSONS IN SYRUP

You might advise anyone eating damsons to beware of the stones because they are maintained whole. For this delectable preserve, it is a small cost to bear.

Swap out the apricots for damsons, but keep the fruits whole. When the skins begin to split, remove the fruit from the syrup and poach it gently. Damsons usually have such a fantastic flavor that adding too many spices will ruin them. In Apricots in Syrup, maintain the orange peel and juice but remove the herbs. Use demerara or high-quality dark brown sugar instead of white sugar because darker sugar will work better with this fruit.

IT MAKES ABOUT 1 PINT

- ¼ scant cup of sugar
- ½ vanilla bean
- approx. 1¼-inch piece of cinnamon stick
- 6 or 7 figs, halved
- ¼ tsp citric acid

FIGS IN VANILLA SYRUP

These lovely, exquisitely pink, jewel-like fruits look fantastic in the jar. The figs will last longer if you bake the pot in the oven.

1. Set the oven to 300 degrees. Add 1 cup of water to the pan with the sugar, cinnamon stick, and vanilla bean. The sugar must first be stirred over low heat to dissolve it, and then it must be brought to a boil and simmered for two minutes to create a syrup. Get rid of the heat. Throw out the cinnamon stick. Using a knife, scrape the vanilla bean seeds and add them to the syrup after slicing it half lengthwise.
2. The sliced sides of the figs should be placed outward when placed in a clean, sterilized jar. Sprinkle the figs with the vanilla bean halves. Swivel the pot to eliminate air bubbles before adding enough syrup to cover the figs in the container.
3. On a baking sheet covered with several layers of folded newspaper, set the jar in the oven with the top of the pot wrapped in aluminum foil. Bake for 25 to 30 minutes, at which point the syrup should have taken on a wonderful pink hue. Seal after taking it out of the oven and removing the foil.

MAKES ABOUT 1 QUART

- Six oranges, cut into ¼-inch slices
- 1¾ cup of white wine vinegar
- 1¼ (rounded) cups of sugar
- ⅓ cup of clear, pale honey
- One small cinnamon stick
- 2 tsp whole coriander seeds
- 1 tsp whole cloves

ORANGE SLICES IN SPICED HONEY

Honey is the sweetener, and various spices flavor the syrup for these orange slices.

Add just enough water to the pan to cover the orange slices. Until the zest is soft, boil and simmer for one hour. Take the water out and throw it away. The sugar and honey should melt after being heated gradually while whisking the remaining ingredients in a skillet. Oranges should be added after simmering for 30 minutes or until the zest is transparent. Then, pack the mixture into sterilized jars. After straining the syrup to remove the spices, add it to the pan and quickly boil it for 10 minutes to decrease it. Fill the jars to the top, then tighten the lids.

MAKES ABOUT 1 QUART

- 2 pounds of small peaches (approx. nine beauties)
- 1¼ (rounded) cups of sugar
- One vanilla bean
- approx. 1 cup of brandy

WHOLE PEACHES IN BRANDY

To use peaches sold off for cheap at the supermarket, preserve them in a brandy syrup. They are frequently solid and flawless but have passed their sell-by date, making them a bargain. Of course, it's best if you cultivate your peaches. They make a beautiful gift that looks amazing when placed inside a jar. It is optional to include a vanilla bean, but doing so is a resourceful way to use up beans that have already had their seeds removed for other recipes. Additionally, the bean looks nice when it is visible through the jar. Adjust the recipe's numbers if you want to use smaller pots since it only yields enough to fill one large jar.

1. Put the peaches in boiling water for a few minutes to skin them. You might have to complete this in groups. Using a sharp knife, the skins of the fruits should come off quickly.
2. Stirring slowly over low heat can help the sugar dissolve when you add 1 cup of water and half of the sugar to a pan. If using, add the vanilla bean after simmering the syrup.
3. The peaches should be added to the syrup in three batches and poached for 5 minutes, with additional syrup spooned on top if necessary. With a slotted spoon, scoop them out and place them in a clean, sterilized jar, neatly packing

them in a while, careful not to crush or damage them. Push the bean down among the fruits after removing it from the syrup.
4. When all the sugar has dissolved, add the remaining sugar to the syrup in the pan and whisk. Increase the heat and boil the mixture quickly for 4 minutes. After 10 minutes, turn off the heat and let the food be excellent.
5. After measuring the syrup and brandy, mix the two ingredients and whisk. After covering the peaches with brandy syrup, cap the jar.

GREENGAGES IN BRANDY

The color and flavor of greengage plums are excellent and work well in this recipe. After serving the fruit, any brandy still in the jar can be sipped as a liqueur. Save every last drop!

Replace the peaches with 2 pounds of firm, ripe greengages in the Whole Peaches in the Brandy recipe. The greengages don't need to be skinned. When poaching the fruits, take care to ensure that they remain whole. If the fruits begin to split, remove them from the syrup right once.

MAKES ABOUT 1 QUART

- 3 cups of ripe cherries
- ⅜ cup of sugar
- 2⅜ cups of eau de vie

CHERRIES IN EAU DE VIE

This must be the most straightforward preservation in the book, yet the little effort required yields an abundant outcome. Serve plain with whipped cream and take pleasure in.

1. Using a cherry stoner, pit the cherries and remove any stalks before putting the fruits with sugar in sterilized, wide-necked jars. Spoon extra sugar on top of the cherries after the jars are full.
2. The eau de vie should cover the cherries in the jars before being sealed. Shake the jars occasionally to help the sugar dissolve and turn into syrup while you store them for at least six weeks.

FRUITS

PRESERVING FRUIT

One of the simplest ways to preserve fresh fruit is to use syrup. After being peeled and sliced into slices, the fruit is put in jars. What kind of syrup you prepare will depend on your preferences. Although it's common, using syrups with a lot of sugar is not technically necessary because the sugar retains the fruit's flavor and texture. You can also use water or unsweetened fruit juice to can fruit, but if you do, know that it won't keep its shape, color, or flavor—and might even appear a little discolored and taste bland—and won't preserve well.

Because heavy syrup is formed from an equal blend of sugar and water, flavoring is straightforward. Mix sugar and water in a large pot to make syrup for fruit and adjust the proportions as needed. The sugar was added to the mixture when brought to a boil. Reduce the heat to a low level and keep the syrup warm before using it. The yield will be between 1 and 2 cups of syrup per quart of fruit.

CANNING FRUIT

If you want to can fruit, start with ripe fruit that is blemish-free or imperfect. Any fresh fruit that is safe to eat raw is appropriate for canning. The bulk of fruits is processed using the same method. The stems should be removed after thorough washing for cherries, berries, peaches, and pears.

With plenty of headspaces, pack the fruit into clean jars. Never pack anything past the first "ring" from the jar's top, according to my rule of thumb (I tell my boys this when they assist me). Pour sugar syrup over the fruit, leaving at least 1 inch of headspace this time. Because canned fruit can boil over and make a sticky mess, prepare it using a straightforward hot water bath canning method. Most fruits should be removed after 20 minutes.

APPLESAUCE

I typically make three bushels of applesauce yearly, the primary fruit I preserve. The Amish usually serve applesauce with every meal except breakfast. It can be served as a side dish with soup or almost anything else. In my house, pizza is served with applesauce. My husband grew up eating it that way, and now our boys like it the same way. I only grin as I see them top their pizza with applesauce. Ginger Gold or other "sweet" apples use less sugar than tart apples like the Smokehouse kind. Smokehouse apples, on the other hand, produce excellent applesauce. You can also choose from a selection of apples to suit your preferences.

YIELD: 1 BUSHEL OF APPLES FOR APPROX. 25 QUARTS

1. Wash apples thoroughly and remove stems. It is not necessary to core or peel the apples using a Victorio strainer. However, it is recommended if you want "clean" applesauce, ideally free of any particles.
2. Fill a large saucepan with water until the bottom is about 2 inches deep.
3. In a pot, add the prepared apples and bring to a boil.
4. Heat until tender and fluffy.
5. Pushing apples carefully through the Victorio food grinder (apples will be heated). The final puree should have a stunning, smooth texture.
6. After the apples have been pureed, add sugar and thoroughly combine.
7. Leave at least a half-inch of headroom when ladling applesauce into jars.
8. Process in a hot water bath for 20 minutes.

BLUEBERRY PIE FILLING

Stocking up on pie-filling cans is a great idea over the winter. Jars of pastry or dessert are exceedingly easy to open.

YIELD: APPROX. 9-10 PINTS

- 3 quarts of fresh blueberries
- 1 quart + 1 cup of cold water, divided
- 3 cups of sugar
- 1½ cups of clear jel
- Mix berries, 1 quart water, and sugar.

1. Bring blueberries, water, and sugar to a boil over medium heat.
2. Mix one cup of chilled water with one clear gel
3. Add to the berry mixture while stirring constantly.
4. Maintain boiling until thick.
5. Transfer to tidy jars.
6. Process in a hot water bath for 20 minutes.

CHERRY PIE FILLING

YIELD: APPROX. 9-10 PINTS

- 7 cups of + 1½ cups of cold water, divided
- 5 cups of sugar
- 3 quarts pitted sour cherries
- 1¾ cups of clear jel

1. Bring 7 cups of water, sugar, and cherries to a boil over medium heat.
2. In a separate bowl, mix 1½ cups of cold water and therm-flo.
3. When adding, thoroughly whisk the cherry mixture until the cherries have thickened.
4. Pour into the jars.
5. For 20 minutes, process in a hot water bath.

APPLE PIE FILLING

YIELD: APPROX. 8-9 PINTS

- 6 cups of + 1 cup of cold water, divided
- 4 cups of sugar
- 1 tbsp cinnamon
- 1¾ cups of clear jel
- 6 quarts of fresh apples, peeled and sliced

1. Bring to a boil 6 cups of water, sugar, and cinnamon.
2. In another pan, mix therm-flo and 1 cup of cold water.
3. As you add the clear gel (therm-Flo) combination to the boiling sugar mixture, stir it continuously.
4. Spoon the combined ingredients over the apples.
5. Transfer to tidy jars.
6. Process in a hot water bath for 20 minutes.

FRUIT PUDDING

Simple and delectable Amish desserts like fruit pudding are eaten independently and with ice cream. Said the juice of your choice has been thickened with therm-flo. You can also add fresh fruit right before serving.

YIELD: APPROX. 9–10 PINTS

- 3 quarts of fruit juice of your choice
- 3 quarts water + extra for therm-flo
- 4 cups of sugar
- 2½ cups of therm-flo

1. I am boiling 3 quarts of water with sugar, fruit juice, and salt.
2. In another bowl, mix them-flo and water to make a smooth paste.
3. While stirring the juice mixture constantly, add the therm flour.
4. Boil the mixture until thick.
5. Pour into tidy jars.
6. Process in a hot water bath for 15 minutes.

CHUTNEYS

Chutney creation is not an exact science, and you can customize it to your preferences by changing the spices and sweetness. Long cooking times are necessary to achieve a rich, thick consistency, but you want to cook it sparingly because it will slightly dry out in storage. Instead, you want a glistening, wet chutney. Chutneys need time to ripen, so be patient.

MAKES ABOUT 4¼ CUPS

- 1 tsp. allspice
- 1 tsp. mustard seeds
- 1 tsp. ground coriander
- One small cinnamon stick
- 1 pound apricots, quartered and stoned
- 1 pound cooking apples, peeled, cored, and chopped into large chunks
- 3 cups of cider or wine vinegar
- 1½ cups of golden raisins, chopped

- Two cloves of garlic, peeled and chopped
- rind and juice of 1 lemon
- 1 tsp. salt
- ¾ -an inch-square piece of fresh ginger root, peeled and minced
- 2 cups of warmed sugar

APRICOT CHUTNEY

Fruit can be used to make this chutney, both fresh and dried. Making the most of a seasonal surplus, this recipe employs fresh apricots. However, you can substitute dried apricots to prepare them outside the season. Use 1⅝ cup of dried apricots soaked in vinegar for a few hours instead of the fresh apricots, and then carry on as usual.

1. Put the spices in a piece of cheesecloth, then tie a string bag around it. Mix the apricots, apples, vinegar, and spice bag in a stainless steel preserving pan. Bring to a boil, then simmer for 10 minutes.
2. The other ingredients should be added and stirred over low heat until all the sugar dissolves. After that, come to a boil and simmer regularly for about 1½ hours or until the chutney is thick but still juicy.
3. Pour the chutney into hot, sterilized jars, then remove the muslin bag before sealing.

APRICOT & ORANGE CHUTNEY

Apricots and oranges go well together. Adding orange makes the chutney even more vivid. This recipe is also helpful because dried apricots may be used at any time of year.

Three large oranges should be used instead of the lemon in apricot chutney. Grate the oranges' zest, remove and discard the white pith, and then coarsely chop the orange meat. Step 2 should now include them. Continue as before.

MAKES ABOUT 9 CUPS

- 2 pounds raw beets, peeled and coarsely grated
- 1 pound of onions, peeled and chopped
- 1½ pounds cooking apples, peeled, cored and chopped
- 3 cups of seedless raisins

- 4½ cups of malt vinegar or spiced pickling vinegar
- Four scant cups of sugar
- 2 tsp. ground ginger

BEET CHUTNEY

Another item that might be overproduced at the height of the season is beets, so preparing chutney is a good use for them.

1. Mix everything in a stainless steel preserving pan to dissolve the sugar and stir over low heat. Bring to a boil, then reduce heat and simmer gently for one hour, occasionally stirring, until the beets and onions are tender and the chutney is thick but not dry.
2. Put the chutney in hot, sterilized jars, then tighten the lids.

MAKES ABOUT 5¼ CUPS

- 1 pound zucchini
- Two rounded tsp. salt, + extra for sprinkling
- 1 pound scarlet runner beans, cut into ¾-inch pieces
- ½ pound corn kernels
- 1 pound onions, minced
- 2¾ cups of cider vinegar
- 1 tbsp. cornstarch
- 1 tbsp. English mustard powder
- 1 tbsp. turmeric
- One green chili, deseeded and minced
- 2 cups of warmed demerara sugar

VEGETABLE GARDEN CHUTNEY

When food grows more quickly than you can, this chutney is a terrific way to use leftover homegrown scraps. Attempt a variety of veggie combos.

Slice the zucchini after cutting it in half lengthwise. Place in a bowl, sprinkle with salt, and sit for an hour. After that, thoroughly rinse and drain the zucchini. Mix all the vegetables and the vinegar in a stainless steel preserving pan. After bringing to a boil, simmer for 10 minutes. Mix the cornstarch, mustard, and turmeric in a bowl with a small amount of the pan's vinegar to make a smooth paste. The paste, chile, and warmed sugar should be added to the pan. Stir over low heat until the sugar has dissolved, then simmer for ¾ to 1 hour, stirring regularly, until the chutney is thick but juicy. As before, pack.

MAKES ABOUT 6 CUPS

- 2 pounds damsons
- 3¾ cups of malt vinegar
- One small cinnamon stick
- One rounded tbsp. allspice
- One scant tsp. cloves
- ½ pound (generous) cooking apples, peeled, cored and chopped
- Two small onions, peeled and minced
- 1½ cups of raisins
- 1½ cups of chopped dates
- 3 cups of (packed) soft brown sugar
- Two small cloves of garlic, peeled and crushed
- 1 tbsp. ground ginger
- 1 tbsp. coarse salt

DAMSON CHUTNEY

This chutney is lovely, dark, and rich. One of my all-time favorite fruits for canning is damson, which gives whatever jam, jelly, chutney, or pickle it contains an outstanding flavor. Even though it is time-consuming, removing the stones is always worthwhile. My preferred method is to boil the fruits before manually removing the stones (usually with the pan on my lap in front of the television). Since damsons only have a fleeting season once a year, it is easy for me to continue this tiresome custom of producing chutney.

1. The damsons should be cooked in a skillet with 1 cup of vinegar until tender and bursting. Remove the stones after they are cold enough to handle. Put the spices in a muslin piece, then tie a string bag around it.
2. Put all the ingredients in a stainless steel preserving pan, boil, and then simmer for 2–2½ hours, occasionally stirring, until the chutney is dark and thick but still juicy.

3. Pour the chutney into hot, sterilized jars, then remove the muslin bag before sealing.

MAKES ABOUT 5¼ CUPS

- 2 pounds green tomatoes
- ½ pound cooking apples, peeled and cored
- 1 pound red onions, roughly chopped
- ¾ cup of rounded (packed) soft brown sugar
- 2½ cups of malt vinegar
- ½ tsp. Mustard seeds
- ½ tsp. cayenne pepper
- 1 tbsp. finely grated fresh ginger root
- 1¼ cups of raisins
- Three green chilies, deseeded and minced
- 1 tsp. salt

GREEN TOMATO & RED ONION CHUTNEY

It is time to bring the last tomatoes inside toward the end of the season when there is no longer enough heat outside to ripen them. There's a risk that the final priceless fruits will gradually turn crimson if you set them on any available vacant windowsill. Another option to slowly ripen them and extend the season is to pack them in boxes and spread them apart in layers with straw or woolen stuff between them; however, if you have an abundance, the still-green ones are ideal for making chutney.

1. To skin the tomatoes, put them in a bowl, cover them with boiling water, and sit for a few seconds. When you cut the fruits with a sharp knife, the skins should quickly come off. When tomatoes are green, it is more difficult to peel them; therefore, steeping them longer than standard bits help. Roughly chop the tomatoes.
2. In a stainless steel preserving pan, mix all the ingredients and bring to a boil. Stirring occasionally, lower the heat, and simmer until everything is prepared and the chutney has thickened.
3. Put the chutney in hot, sterilized jars, then tighten the lids.

MAKES ABOUT 5¼ CUPS

- 2 pounds mango flesh, when peeled and stoned (about 4 pounds unstoned)

- 2 tsp. mixed pickling spices
- juice and thickly pared rind of 1 small orange
- ½ pound onions, minced
- 1¼ cups of white wine vinegar
- Two cloves garlic
- 1 tbsp. grated ginger root
- Two hot red chilies, deseeded and minced
- 2⅜ cups of (packed) warmed good-quality light brown sugar

MANGO CHUTNEY

This sticky, sweet chutney is the perfect complement to Indian meals. If you are still determining if your mangoes are ripe enough to eat, like I am, this is a great way to use them while they are still a little underripe.

1. Leave the remaining half of the mango flesh in larger chunks and cut the first half into little pieces. Put the rind pieces and pickling spices in a bit of muslin, then tie the amount of fabric into a bag.
2. In a stainless steel preserving pan, mix all the ingredients, excluding the sugar and the large mango chunks, and boil gently for 20 minutes until the mango and onions are tender.
3. Continue to boil for 5 minutes after adding the remaining mango gently. Then, while stirring gently and carefully preserving the chunky texture, cook the mixture until it achieves a thick, jam-like consistency. Add the warmed sugar and stir over low heat until it completely dissolves.
4. Take out the muslin bag. After 10 minutes, mix the chutney once more to spread the chunks.
5. Put the chutney in hot, sterilized jars, then tighten the lids.

MAKES ABOUT 5½ CUPS

- 2¼ pounds nectarines, skinned, stoned, and roughly chopped
- ½ pound cooking apples, peeled, cored, and chopped
- ½ pound onions, peeled and finely sliced
- 1½ cups of raisins
- 1½ cups of (packed) light brown sugar
- 3 tbsp. stem ginger, minced

- Two cloves garlic
- 2 tsp. coarse salt
- 1 tsp. cayenne pepper
- 1 pint white wine vinegar

NECTARINE CHUTNEY

The nectarine works so nicely in this. This recipe is one of my favorites because it has the perfect balance of sweetness and acidity to make a fantastic chutney. I enjoy it on a sandwich with almost anything, especially macaroni cheese!

1. Mix all the ingredients in a stainless steel preserving pan to dissolve the sugar and stir over low heat. Gently simmer for about 1½ hours, stirring periodically, until the chutney is thick but still juicy.
2. Put the chutney in hot, sterilized jars, then tighten the lids.

EVERY CHUTNEY

Nectarines can be replaced by peaches here directly and respectfully. Use whatever is available in large quantities, and you won't be disappointed.

Use peaches instead of nectarines in the Nectarine Chutney recipe. Pick fruits that are firm and just beginning to ripen.

MAKES ABOUT 4 CUPS

- 2 pounds onions, peeled and finely sliced
- Two scant tbsp. olive oil
- 1 pint red wine vinegar
- 3 cups of (packed) good-quality brown sugar
- Two bay leaves
- 15–18 black peppercorns, crushed
- Two scant tsp. salt

ONION MARMALADE

Onion marmalade, more of chutney or relish and not a marmalade, has recently gained enormous popularity in Britain. Generally speaking, it could be better, but this particular chutney will.

1. Cut the onion rings from the slices. The onion rings should be tender but not browned after being gently cooked for about 20 minutes in oil in a stainless steel preserving pan.
2. When the marmalade is black and thick but still juicy, add the remaining ingredients and boil slowly for 1–1½ hours, stirring regularly.
3. Put the jam in hot, sterilized jars, then tighten the lids.

MAKES ABOUT 6¼ CUPS

- 1 tsp. whole allspice
- 1 tsp. coriander seeds
- 2 tsp. Mustard seeds
- ½ tsp. cumin seeds
- Two pieces of fresh root ginger, approx. ¾ × 2½ inches, bruised
- 3¼ pounds red tomatoes, skinned and chopped
- 1 pound cooking apples, peeled, cored, and diced
- 1 pound onions, peeled and minced
- Two small cloves of garlic, peeled and minced
- 1 cup of red wine vinegar
- 1 tsp. coarse salt
- ⅞ cup of (packed) warmed good-quality brown sugar

RED TOMATO & GARLIC CHUTNEY

Another straightforward classic that makes use of an abundance of tomatoes. Chutney is so simple to prepare that it's amazing anyone ever buys the pre-made variety. In this case, the chutney has a nice, deep color thanks to the red fruits and brown sugar.

1. Put the whole spices and ginger bruised in a piece of muslin and secure it with string to form a bag.
2. Mix all the ingredients except the sugar in a stainless steel preserving pan. Bring to a boil, then simmer for a certain amount of time until the vegetables are fork-tender. Add the warmed sugar and continue stirring over low heat when all the sugar has dissolved. Turn to raise the heat, boil, then simmer gently for about ½ hour, stirring periodically, until the chutney is thick but not dry.
3. Pour the chutney into hot, sterilized jars, then remove the muslin bag before sealing.

HOT TOMATO, APPLE, & CHILI CHUTNEY

Adding some extra spices and red hot chilies, this recipe's variant packs a powerful punch. Delicious. Add some to the pasta.

Follow the directions for Red Tomato and Garlic Chutney and add three deseeded and minced spicy red chilies. You may also add five whole cardamom seeds, spices, and a couple of garlic cloves.

MAKES ABOUT 5 CUPS

- 2 pounds apples, peeled and cored
- 2½ cups of cider vinegar
- ⅜ cup of pickling spice
- 1 tbsp. ground ginger
- 1½ cups of raisins
- 2 (packed) cups of warmed brown sugar
- 2 tsp. salt
- One red chili, deseeded and minced

AUNT EDNA'S APPLE CHUTNEY

This was the first chutney I had ever prepared, and was handed to me by a friend's aunt in the 1970s. The outcomes are trustworthy, and I've succeeded numerous times subsequently. I'm grateful, Aunt Edna.

1. In a stainless steel preserving pan, mix the apples and vinegar. Put cheesecloth in the pan and tie the ground ginger and pickling spice together with string. Cook apples gently until they are soft but still maintain their structure.
2. The raisins should be roughly chopped or processed in a food processor before being added to the pan, along with the sugar, salt, and optional chile. When the chutney is thickened but still juicy, take it from the heat after bringing it to a boil. Take out the spice bag.
3. Put the chutney in hot, sterilized jars, then tighten the lids.

IT MAKES ABOUT 5 CUPS

- 2 pounds of cooking apples, peeled, cored and chopped
- 4½ cups of malt vinegar

- ½ pound onions, peeled and chopped
- Two scant tsp. mustard seeds
- One scant tsp. ground ginger
- 1½ light cups of warmed brown sugar
- 1¾ cups of chopped dried dates
- One clove of garlic, peeled and chopped

APPLE & DATE CHUTNEY

Even though I only have one small crab apple tree, I end up with bags of apples every autumn. Another recipe to use up the fruit is fantastic because friends always have more than they can eat of it.

In a stainless steel preserving pan, mix the first five ingredients. Bring to a boil, then simmer for a few minutes or until the apples are mushy but retain some shape. Then turn off the fire and whisk in the dates, sugar, and garlic over low heat until the sugar is dissolved. Increase the heat, boil, reduce the heat, and simmer the chutney until it is thick but not dry. As before, pack.

IT MAKES ABOUT 6½ CUPS

- 12 peppercorns
- 2 tsp. whole allspice
- ¾-inch-square piece of fresh ginger root, bruised
- 5½ cups of pumpkin flesh, cut into ⅝-inch cubes (from pumpkin weighing approx. 2¾ pounds)
- 1 pound cooking apples, peeled, cored, and finely chopped
- Two rounded tbsp. minced stem ginger
- ¾ pound shallots, peeled, cored, and minced
- 1⅜ cup of golden raisins, chopped
- Two cloves of garlic, minced
- 2 tsp. salt
- 2½ cups of cider vinegar
- 1⅞ cups of (packed) warmed soft brown sugar

PUMPKIN CHUTNEY

Pumpkins and squashes are always visually appealing, with fantastic shapes, textures, and brilliant hues. Their flesh gives this chutney a colorful appearance and sweeter flavor, which is always lovely.

1. Put the gingerroot, dry spices, and muslin in a bag and secure it with twine. In a stainless steel preserving pan, mix all the ingredients (apart from the sugar) and slowly bring to a boil. The pumpkin and apple should be soft after a gentle simmer for 20 minutes.
2. While simmering for about 1–1½ hours, occasionally stirring, until the chutney is thick but still juicy, add the warmed sugar and mix until all the sugar has dissolved.
3. Pour the chutney into hot, sterilized jars, then remove the muslin bag before sealing.

MARROW SQUASH CHUTNEY

Finding "excellent ways with marrow squash" is essential since those who cultivate them frequently find themselves with an abundance of enormous specimens and no idea what to do with them. Marrow squash is a helpful "filler-outer" in preserving, particularly chutneys, much like apples. They are a pretty watery vegetable, so you'll need to drain some of it at the beginning to concentrate the flavor.

Pumpkin Chutney can be made using the same quantity of marrow squash instead of pumpkin. The stem ginger is not necessary to add. To drain the excess water from the squash, place it in a basin with some salt and let it sit for 12 hours. Then, rinse it well, pat it dry, and proceed as directed above.

IT MAKES ABOUT 5½ CUPS

- 3 pounds of pears, peeled, cored, and cut into chunks
- 1 pound of onions, peeled and chopped
- grated rind and juice of 1 lemon
- grated rind and juice of 1 orange
- One scant cup of sugar
- 1½ light cups of seedless raisins
- 1¼ cup of cider vinegar

- 1 tsp. salt
- 1 tsp. ground ginger
- ½ tsp. cloves

PEAR CHUTNEY

The amount of fruitiness and spice in this chutney is just ideal. Although this pear chutney is no exception, I typically advise leaving chutney in the cupboard for a few months before using it. However, it does taste astonishingly excellent right away. If you can, save it for a while; otherwise, eat it up and savor it! With cheese, it is perfect.

1. Add the ingredients to a stainless steel preserving pan when all the sugar has dissolved and stir over low heat. Stirring regularly, boil, then reduce heat and simmer for about two hours or until the chutney is dark, thick, and juicy. It will thicken slightly as it cools, as with all chutneys.
2. Put the chutney in hot, sterilized jars, then tighten the lids.

CURDS

These little fruity pots are incredible. I prepare different curds and serve them in tiny sweet pastry casings in tsp-sized dollops. Everyone can be enjoyed with appropriate ceremony and savored over in conversation. Fruit curds don't last as long as jams, yet they still won't be around long enough.

MAKES ABOUT 3 CUPS

- One vanilla bean
- 1¼ pounds crab apples, halved,
- One stick of butter, preferably unsalted, cut into cubes
- 1⅞ cups of refined granulated sugar
- Three large eggs + 2 egg yolks, beaten

CRAB APPLE & VANILLA CURD

Any crisp apple would work just as well; crab apples offer the perfect tartness to give this curd lots of flavor. Windfalls can be utilized, if wanted, more or less as they are because the fruit has been puréed, so little preparation is required (just with any bad bits removed). The most fantastic filling for a sweet pastry case is made from this curd.

1. The vanilla bean should be split lengthwise and added to the pan with the apples and 1 tbsp water. Gently simmer the apples for a few minutes until they are mushy, stirring regularly to prevent the fruit from sticking to the pan's bottom. It should be taken off the fire and allowed to cool.
2. After removing the vanilla bean, purée the apples by running them through a food mill's fine disk or a sieve, then place the finished purée in a bowl. Remove the seeds from the vanilla bean pieces with a sharp knife and mix them with the bean in the apples. While passing the egg through a sieve, combine the remaining ingredients.
3. Use a double boiler or place the bowl over a pan of simmering water to gradually cook the mixture while constantly stirring until all the ingredients are combined and the curd thickens and coats the back of the spoon. This phase should last 20 to 30 minutes.
4. Take out the vanilla bean fragments. Fill small, heated, sterilized jars with the hot curd, then seal them.

IT MAKES ABOUT 1½ CUPS

- ½ pound apricots, quartered and stoned
- Two eggs, well beaten
- zest and juice of 1 lemon
- 3 tbsp (slightly rounded) butter, preferably unsalted, cut into cubes
- One scant cup of refined granulated sugar

APRICOT CURD

Even commercially cultivated apricots from the grocery store will yield delicious curd, but fresh apricots from your backyard cannot be beaten. When creating curds, use the highest-quality organic eggs possible because they contribute to the finished product's brighter color.

1. Cook the apricots gently until tender in a skillet with 2 tbsp water (just enough to prevent the fruit from sticking to the pan's bottom).
2. The fruit should be cooled before being pressed through a food mill's fine disk or a sieve, collecting the purée in a basin.
3. Put the purée through a sieve with the beaten eggs in it. Butter, sugar, and lemon juice should all be added.

4. Over a pot of hot water, place the bowl. Simmer the mixture, constantly swirling with a wooden spoon, until it is thoroughly combined and has thickened enough to coat the back of the spoon. It should take 30 minutes or so.
5. Seal the small, hot, sterilized jars after adding the curd.

IT MAKES ABOUT 1 CUP

- 1-pint raspberries
- ⅝ (rounded) cup of refined granulated sugar
- 3 tbsp butter, preferably unsalted, cut into cubes
- Two tiny eggs, beaten

RASPBERRY CURD

Raspberries contribute to this delicious curd's gorgeous color and delightfully acidic flavor. Save tiny glass jars of odd shapes specifically for creating curds. They make lovely presents.

1. Squash the raspberries with a spoon to help release the juice as you simmer them gently for 5 to 10 minutes.
2. Puréed fruit is collected in a bowl after being forced through a sieve.
3. Then, after pouring the beaten eggs through a sieve onto the purée, set the bowl over a pan of hot water. Until everything is thoroughly combined, stir with a wooden spoon. It should take 20 to 30 minutes to cook until the curd thickens enough to coat the back of a spoon while constantly stirring.
4. Seal the small, hot, sterilized jars after adding the curd.

IT MAKES ABOUT 2 CUPS

- 1-pint blueberries
- zest and juice of 1 large lime
- 4 tbsp butter, preferably unsalted, cut into cubes
- 1⅛ cups of refined granulated sugar
- Two large eggs, beaten

BLUEBERRY & LIME CURD

The best and sweetest blueberries tend to be on the wrong side, and in this recipe, lime juice and zest give the berries an extra flavor boost.

When the blueberries are soft, add them to a skillet with the lime zest and juice and simmer them gently for 5 to 10 minutes. The fruit should be puréed before continuing with Raspberry Curd stages 2-4.

IT MAKES ABOUT 2 CUPS

- 1-pint gooseberries, with any large stems removed
- zest of 1 lime
- 6 tbsp + 1 tsp butter, preferably unsalted, cut into cubes
- ⅞ cup of refined granulated sugar
- Three large eggs + 2 yolks, beaten

GOOSEBERRY CURD

Although gooseberries are not usually readily available in American grocery stores, they are straightforward to grow and don't require much care to thrive. Consider increasing some to make this curd.

1. Squash the gooseberries with a spoon to help release the juice and cook them gently for 5–10 minutes in a pan with ⅜ cup of water.
2. To remove the fruit's skins and seeds and to purée it, run it through a food mill's fine disk. Collect the purée in a bowl.
3. Then, after pouring the beaten eggs through a sieve onto the purée, set the bowl over a pan of hot water. It should take 20 to 30 minutes to thoroughly combine, smooth, and thicken everything to the point where the back of a wooden spoon may be coated.
4. Fill hot, sterilized jars with the curd, then seal them.

IT MAKES ABOUT 1¼ CUPS

- zest and juice of 3 lemons
- 6 tbsp butter, preferably unsalted, cut into cubes
- ⅞ cup of refined granulated sugar
- Three large eggs, beaten

LEMON CURD

This tart lemon curd is a superb classic that is ideal as the filling for an open tart. It can also be incorporated into vanilla ice cream or put between the layers of a cake. No matter how you serve it, it is absolute perfection.

1. Put the butter, sugar, and lemon juice in a bowl and place it over a pan of simmering water. Pour the beaten eggs through a sieve before adding them.
2. Using a wooden spoon, stir the mixture until it is well cooked and combined. It should take around 15 to 20 minutes to cook until the curd thickens enough to coat the back of the spoon while constantly stirring
3. Seal the small, hot, sterilized jars with the curd.

IT MAKES ABOUT 1 CUP

- zest and juice of 3 Seville oranges
- 3 tbsp (slightly rounded) butter, preferably unsalted, cut into cubes
- ¾ cup of refined granulated sugar
- Two large eggs, beaten

BITTER ORANGE CURD

A curd benefits significantly from the Seville oranges' bitter flavor. Most sweet oranges simply lack the personality to be used this way, while blood oranges work just as well because they pack a more pungent taste punch than other sweet varieties. Spread the curd liberally between the layers of a rich chocolate cake, use it as the filling for a sweet pastry tart, or serve it on a thick slice of fresh bread.

Utilizing the components listed above, make lemon curd according to the recipe.

IT MAKES ABOUT 1¼ CUPS

- zest of 2 small grapefruit
- 6 tbsp grapefruit juice
- 6 tbsp butter, preferably unsalted, cut into cubes
- ⅞ cup of refined granulated sugar
- Three large eggs, beaten

GRAPEFRUIT CURD

Here is yet another citrus take on lemon curd. Although this card is silky and creamy, it has a unique tang.

Utilizing the components listed above, make lemon curd according to the recipe.

IT MAKES ABOUT 1½ CUPS

- One small butternut squash peeled, deseeded, and roughly chopped
- zest and juice of 1 lemon
- zest and juice of 1 orange
- 4 tbsp + 1 tsp butter, preferably unsalted, cut into cubes
- ⅞ cup of refined granulated sugar
- Two large eggs + 2 yolks, beaten
- Four pieces of stem ginger, approx. 1 inch in diameter, finely chopped
- 3 tbsp syrup from the stem ginger

BUTTERNUT & GINGER CURD

Because they are naturally sweet, pumpkins and squash are perfect for producing sweet preserves. The main ingredient in this dish is butternut squash, but you may also use other varieties. The flesh should be an intense orange color. The texture is given an excellent bite by chopped stem ginger.

1. To prevent the squash from sticking to the pan as it cooks, place it in a pan with ½ cup of water. Cook with the lid on until the food is mushy, then drain any extra liquid.
2. The squash can be processed into a smooth paste in a food processor or through a food mill's fine disk. You might also pass it through a sieve.
3. Measure 1¼ cups of the squash purée, mix it with the remaining ingredients in a bowl set over hot water, and then pour the beaten eggs over the purée. It should take around 30 minutes to thoroughly mix everything, completely dissolve the sugar, and thicken the curd until it coats the back of the wooden spoon.
4. Seal the small, hot, sterilized jars after adding the curd.

TOMATOES

A WORD ABOUT TOMATO PRODUCTS WITH LEMON JUICE:

Food safety organizations recommend adding 1 and 2 tbsp of bottled lemon juice to every pint and quart of tomato product, respectively. I've never added lemon juice to my tomato products and haven't had a problem, but if you'd like to, you can do it as an additional safety precaution.

A NOTE ON THERM-FLO:

Therm-Flo, a modified food starch, is a thickening agent in canning recipes. Usually, it is thickened, added to tomato products, and turned into a paste with water. If you prefer to avoid adding starch to your product, tomato paste is another option for thickening home-canned tomato products. Therm-flow is always available in Amish or Mennonite bulk food and grocery stores, and I'm sure it's also available online.

STEWED TOMATOES

YIELD: THIS RECIPE CAN BE ADAPTED TO ANY SIZE JAR.

- tomatoes, enough to fill your jar of choice
- One heaping tbsp chopped onion
- One heaping tbsp chopped green peppers
- One heaping tbsp chopped celery
- 1 tbsp sugar
- One tsp salt

1. Cut the tomato in half and skin it.
2. Fill jars with tomatoes.
3. Fill every quart with the remaining ingredients.
4. Process in a hot water bath for an hour.

HOT SAUCE

YIELD: APPROX. 2-4 PINTS

- 1 pound tomatoes
- 1 pound of hot peppers of your choice
- 1 pound onions

- One tsp salt
- ½ cup of white vinegar
- One tsp of garlic salt

1. Wash and chop the tomatoes, onions, and peppers.
2. Mix with the remaining components and bring to a boil.
3. Cook until soft.
4. Push through a Victorio strainer or a tomato press.
5. Scoop into containers.
6. Process in a hot water bath for 30 minutes.

TOMATO SOUP

Using this recipe, condensed soup is produced. Before serving, add an equal amount of milk. This was a typical family lunch that my mother would make. It pairs well with grilled cheese and has a mild flavor.

YIELD: APPROX. 8–10 QUARTS

- 14 quarts of tomatoes, sliced
- 3 quarts + 2 quarts water divided
- Seven medium onions
- 14 stalks celery
- 14 sprigs parsley
- 2 cups of flour
- 3 cups of brown sugar
- ½ cup of salt
- 1 cup of butter, melted

1. In 3 quarts of water, soften the tomatoes.
2. In 2 quarts of water, soften the celery, onions, and parsley. Vegetables must be sufficiently soft to fit through a Victorio strainer or food mill.
3. Add the juice from the strained cooked vegetables to a sizable stockpot.
4. Mix the flour, salt, and brown sugar in a bowl.
5. Stir in enough cold water and melted butter to make a thick slurry resembling cake batter.
6. Continue to whisk as you add the flour to the tomato juice mixture.

7. Turn up the heat and let the water boil for a minute.
8. Ladle into jars and process for one hour in a hot water bath.

CHILI BASE

YIELD: APPROX. 20 PINTS

- 12 quarts of tomatoes, peeled
- 12 onions, chopped
- Two bunches of celery, chopped
- 1 cup of salt
- 3 cups of vinegar
- 7 cups of sugar
- Three peppers or more as needed, chopped
- 1 tbsp black pepper or more as needed
- 1 tbsp cinnamon or more as needed
- 1 tbsp allspice or more as needed
- 1 tbsp ginger or more as needed

1. Mix tomatoes, celery, onions, and salt.
2. Allow to stand at room temperature for eight hours or overnight.
3. Include the remaining ingredients.
4. Heat till boiling.
5. Distribute to jars.
6. Take a 30-minute hot-water bath to finish the treatment.

(BASIC) TOMATO JUICE

You can easily modify this recipe to suit your preferences or needs. A more upscale variation of this simple dish.

YIELD: APPROX. 3 POUNDS OF TOMATOES FOR 1-QUART JUICE

1. Heat the tomatoes until soft enough to pass through a food mill.
2. Bring tomato juice to a boil and season as needed.
3. Put portions into jars.
4. Process in a hot water bain-marie for 15 minutes.

SEASONED TOMATO JUICE

YIELD: APPROX. 4–6 QUARTS

- ½ bushel tomatoes
- 5–6 bell peppers
- Three large onions
- Seven stalks of celery
- ¼ cup of salt

1. Slice the vegetables.
2. Bring to a boil.
3. Prepare the food until soft enough to pass through a Victorio sieve.
4. A salted liquid that has reached a rolling boil
5. Scoop into containers.
6. Process in a hot water bath for 15 minutes.

HOMEMADE V-8 JUICE

YIELD: 6 QUARTS

- 6 quarts of tomato juice
- ¾ cup of sugar
- Two tsp of onion salt or more as needed
- Two tsp of garlic salt or more as needed
- Two tsp of celery salt or more as needed
- One tsp of salt or more as needed
- ½ tsp pepper

1. Bring all ingredients to a boil.
2. Pour into the jars.
3. Process in a hot water bath for 30 minutes.

PIZZA SAUCE (VARIATION 1)

I prepare this dish every summer. I also use it to create spaghetti or lasagna in addition to pizza. View different pizza sauce recipes.

YIELD: APPROX. 6-7 PINTS

- 9 pounds of fresh tomatoes
- ½ cup of lemon juice, new or bottled,
- Two tsp of dried oregano or more as needed
- One tsp of ground black pepper
- One tsp of salt
- One tsp of garlic powder

1. Cut off stems and thoroughly wash tomatoes.
2. Add one inch or so of water to a large stockpot.
3. Quarter the tomatoes, then thoroughly reheat.
4. Bring tomatoes to a boil for three to five minutes or until they soften.
5. Pass softened tomatoes through a food processor, tomato press,
6. Fill a large stockpot with ingredients and tomato sauce.
7. Boil while occasionally stirring until the sauce is thin.
8. Ladle into jars and process in a hot water bath for 30 minutes.

PIZZA SAUCE (VARIATION 2)

YIELD: APPROX. 10 PINTS

- 2½ gallons of diced tomatoes
- 8–10 medium onions
- Four green peppers
- 2 cups of vegetable oil
- ½ gallon tomato paste + more as needed
- 1 cup of sugar
- 2 tbsp oregano
- Two tsp pepper
- 3 tbsp pizza seasoning
- 1 tbsp Italian seasoning
- 2 tbsp dried basil
- One tsp of garlic powder
- ½ cup of salt
- Therm-Flo,

1. Bring the tomatoes, onions, and peppers to a boil in a large stockpot.
2. Boiling for 20 minutes.
3. Pass through a tomato press or Victorio strainer.
4. After adding the purée to a large stockpot, add the following ingredients.
5. Boil for an hour nonstop.
6. Add more tomato paste to the sauce if it needs to be thickened.
7. Ladle into jars and process in a hot water bath for 30 minutes.

PIZZA SAUCE (VARIATION 3)

YIELD: APPROX. 6–7 PINTS

- 6 quarts of tomato juice
- 1 tbsp garlic
- 1 tbsp oregano
- 1½ tsp black pepper
- 2 tbsp salt
- 2 cups of sugar
- One package of Mrs. Wages Pizza Sauce Tomato Mix
- 1 cup of therm-flo

1. Mix all the ingredients in a large stockpot, excluding the therm-flo.
2. Boiling for 30 minutes is
3. Mix therm-flo and water to make a paste.
4. While continuously stirring, add the tomato-flour mixture to the tomato mixture.
5. Maintain boiling until thick.
6. Ladle into jars and process for 30 minutes in a hot water bath.

KETCHUP (VARIATION 1)

Homemade ketchup has an entirely distinct flavor from store-bought. It usually has a thinner consistency and a sweeter taste for a different take on this ketchup recipe.

YIELD: APPROX. 8–10 PINTS

- 4 quarts of tomato juice
- 2¼ cups of sugar

- One tsp of pepper
- ¾ tsp allspice
- 1½ tsp onion powder
- ¾ tsp cinnamon
- ¾ tsp cloves
- 1 tbsp salt
- 2 cups of vinegar
- 1½ cups of therm-flo

1. Mix all the ingredients in a large stockpot, excluding the therm-flo.
2. After coming to a boil, continue to boil for 15 minutes.
3. Create a paste by combining therm-flo with a tiny amount of water.
4. While continuously stirring, add the tomato-flour mixture to the tomato mixture.
5. Maintain boiling until thick.
6. Ladle into jars and process for 30 minutes in a hot water bath.

KETCHUP (VARIATION 2)

YIELD: APPROX. 6–7 PINTS

- 4 quarts of tomato juice
- ¾ cup of brown sugar
- ¾ cup of white sugar
- Two tsp of dry mustard
- One tsp of ginger
- One tsp of celery seed
- One tsp of pepper
- 1½ tsp salt
- ½ tsp cayenne pepper
- ¾ cup of vinegar
- ¾ cup of therm-flo

1. Mix all the ingredients in a large stockpot, excluding the therm-flo.
2. After coming to a boil, continue to cook for an hour.
3. Mix therm-flo and water to make a paste.

4. Add while continuously stirring the tomato mixture.
5. Maintain boiling until thick.
6. Ladle into jars and process for 30 minutes in a hot water bath.

SALSA (VARIATION 1)

YIELD: APPROX. 12–15 PINTS

- 4–5 quarts of tomatoes, peeled, chopped
- Four large onions, chopped
- 1½ cups of jalapeños (approx. six peppers), chopped
- Six bell peppers, chopped
- 2 cups of white vinegar
- 1½ tbsp chili powder
- ½ tsp alum
- ½ cup of pickling salt
- 1 tbsp garlic powder
- One tsp of onion powder
- 4½ tsp pepper
- ⅓ cup of sugar
- 1 (12-oz.) can of tomato paste

1. Mix everything but the tomato paste and the therm-flo.
2. Bring to a boil in a big stockpot.
3. Simmering for three minutes.
4. To make the salsa thicker, you can add tomato paste.
5. Ladle into jars and process for 20 minutes in a hot water bath.

SALSA (VARIATION 2)

YIELD: APPROX. 7–8 PINTS

- 14 cups of peeled and chopped tomatoes
- 3 cups of chopped onions
- ½ cup of chopped jalapeño peppers
- 2½ cups of chopped bell peppers
- ¼ cup of salt

- Four tsp of chili powder
- Four tsp cumin
- 1 cup of tomato sauce
- 3 tbsp brown sugar
- 6 tbsp therm-flo
- ⅔ cup of vinegar

1. Mix the peppers, onions, and tomatoes.
2. Seasonings are added; mix well.
3. Mix tomato sauce, brown sugar, and therm flour.
4. Pour the mixture after thoroughly stirring the vegetables.
5. Include the vinegar and mix well.
6. Boil the mixture for 20 minutes,
7. Ladle into jars and process for 20 minutes in a hot water bath.

PICKLES

Pickles' main component is vinegar, which is also their main flavoring. Here, vinegar shines; the more seasoned and seasoned it is, the better. You can use any vinegar. However, cider vinegar pairs well with fruits like apples and pears, malt vinegar goes well with darker pickles, and white wine vinegar enhances the color of ingredients.

IT MAKES ABOUT 2¼ CUPS

- 2 pounds of crab apples
- 2¾ cups of cider
- One small cinnamon stick
- Nine cloves
- One scant tsp allspice
- 3 cups of warmed sugar

SPICED CRAB APPLE PICKLE

Crab apples are beautiful due to their small size when used whole, as they are in this pickle. The appearance of the spot will vary greatly depending on the type of apple used, with little ruby red apples having a particularly adorable appearance.

Allow a few pickled apples for every serving while keeping the apple whole and leaving the stems on. The apples must be pristine before you begin because they require so little preparation, even though they are awkward small fruits. If crab apples aren't available, you can use other apple varieties for this pickle. Larger fruits should be cored, chopped, and pickled like smaller pieces. When paired with cheese and biscuits, this pickle is excellent.

1. Use a darning needle to prick the apple skins.
2. In a stainless steel pan, mix the vinegar with the spices, bring to a boil, then reduce the heat and simmer for five minutes. The apples should be added and simmered until they are soft but retain shape. Using a slotted spoon, carefully remove them from the vinegar and place them in hot, sterilized jars.
3. Warm the sugar, then add it to the vinegar and stir until all of the sugar has dissolved. Increase the heat and boil the mixture until the vinegar has decreased by about a third and is sticky.
4. Seal the jars after covering the apples entirely with the boiling syrup.

IT MAKES ABOUT 3 CUPS

- 1-pint cider vinegar
- 2 cups of sugar
- juice and zest pared from 1 lemon, cut into chunks
- Five whole allspice berries
- 2-star anise
- Two dried red chilies
- Five black peppercorns
- 3¼ pounds pears

PICKLED PEARS

This pickle looks just gorgeous. The pears go wonderfully with cheese and make a great relish to serve with cold cuts. Make a salad dressing with any leftover sweet, spicy vinegar in the jar and sprinkle it over a salad with goat cheese.

1. Mix the vinegar, sugar, lemon peel pieces, and spices in a stainless steel pan. Stir over low heat until the sugar is dissolved. To keep the pears from turning brown, peel and cut them into quarters before putting them in the lemon juice.

2. Depending on the fruit's ripe, place the pears in the spiced syrup and simmer them gently for about 30 minutes or until they are soft and transparent. Remove the pear pieces and put them in clean jars using a slotted spoon.
3. Pour the syrup and spices over the pears, ensuring they are entirely submerged after boiling them in the pan to reduce it by half. Allow to cool, then seal.

IT MAKES ABOUT 1¾ CUPS

- Three plums, halved and stoned
- Two apricots, halved and stoned
- 2 figs, halved
- Two small pears, peeled and quartered
- 1¾ cups of sugar
- juice of 1 lemon
- ⅝ cup of dry white wine
- One generous cup of honey
- ½ cup of (scant) English mustard powder

MOSTARDA DI FRUTTA

This is a fantastic time to get acquainted with mustard fruits if you aren't already. It is a delectable Italian condiment with a mustard base. (In actuality, the word derives from most, the unfermented grape juice thickened to a syrup in which the fruits were stored initially, not from "mustard"). It can be made with any combination of fruits but is typically made with pears, plums, peaches, whole cherries, and figs—the original recipe called for quinces or grapes.

When served sliced over the fish, this pickle pairs well with pork, sausages, spicy, salty cheeses, and fish. Mostarda can be blended with pumpkin and finely diced to produce a ravioli filling. Any syrup that is left over can be used for salad dressings and drizzled over bitter salad greens.

1. The oven to 250 degrees Fahrenheit. Add just enough water to cover the fruit in a stainless steel pan.
2. Gently stir the sugar and lemon juice to dissolve, then increase the heat and boil to create a thin syrup. Spend 10 minutes on low heat to cook the fruit pieces while keeping them whole.

3. With a slotted spoon, remove the fruit pieces, thoroughly drain them, and arrange them on a baking sheet. The fruits should be dried after 45 to 50 minutes in the oven.
4. To decrease the syrup, mix it with the wine and honey and cook it for 10 to 15 minutes at a low temperature. Stir in the mustard powder thoroughly.
5. Pour the syrup over the fruit pieces in hot, sterilized jars to cover. Allow to cool, then seal.

IT MAKES ABOUT 1¾ CUPS

- 1 pound damsons
- One scant cup of sugar
- Two short cinnamon sticks
- Six cloves
- Four pieces of gingerroot, about ¾-inch square
- malt vinegar

PICKLED DAMSONS

It's worth the effort to pickle damsons using this traditional approach. Even if the pickle weren't quite as rich, reducing the filtering and boiling would still be great.

1. Set the oven to 300 degrees. Add sugar and place the damson in a ceramic dish. Wrap the spices with muslin and tie them. When the fruit feels mushy, and the juices begin to run, pour enough vinegar over it to cover it, sprinkle the bag of spices, and then place the dish in the bottom of the oven for 20 minutes.
2. Allow the juice to cool before straining it into a pan and adding the spices. Pour the liquid over the damsons after boiling it and removing the spices. After performing this straining and boiling procedure (without adding any spices) daily for ten days, leave the damsons submerged in the juice for an additional seven days, refrigerating in between.
3. Damsons should be strained and placed in a hot, sterilized jar. Pour over the damsons after boiling the syrupy, rich juice. When it is cold, seal the container.

IT MAKES ABOUT 1¾ CUPS

- 1 pound apricots
- One scant cup of sugar
- Two short cinnamon sticks

- Two cloves
- Two pieces of gingerroot, about ¾-inch square
- ½ tsp whole allspice
- wine vinegar

PICKLED APRICOTS

This is another versatile option in which the vinegar's pungency properly balances the fruit's sweetness. Use dried apricots instead of fresh ones when they aren't in season.

Use the apricots and various spice quantities as in Step 1 above. With a slotted spoon, remove the apricots and place them in a sterilized jar. Pour the syrupy liquid over the apricots after bringing the remaining liquid to a boil and removing the spice bag. Place overnight in the refrigerator. The following morning, take the apricots out of the jar and pour the syrup into a pan. Replacing the apricots in the pot, bringing the syrup to a boil, and then pouring it over the fruit. Allow to cool, then seal.

IT MAKES ABOUT 3 PINTS

- Nine small lemons
- coarse salt
- One bay leaf
- One small cinnamon stick
- a few coriander seeds
- One dried chili

PRESERVED LEMONS

Lemons that have been preserved are crucial in Moroccan and North African cuisines. They have a fragrant, sweet, and sour flavor and can be used in salads and casseroles. The entire fruit, rind, can be consumed after being pickled. Replenish the jar with salt and lemon juice to submerge the fruits when the lemons are used.

1. Every lemon should have the stalk end removed before being quartered to within ¾ inch of the base so that it opens out but stays together.

2. The lemons should be packed as tightly as possible into a big (about 1 quart), sterilized wide-necked jar. Pushing the lemons down will help them release their juice. Pack the salt between the cuts, using about 1 tbsp for every lemon. Place the remaining flavorings, which should be left whole, among the lemons. Overnight, seal the jar and leave it.
3. The following day, squeeze the lemons harder to extract additional juice. Do this daily over three days, adding extra lemon juice until the lemons are completely covered in liquid.
4. Close the jar. The lemons should be tender and ready to use once a month has passed.
5. The lemons can be kept for at least six months in the refrigerator. Before usage, remove extra salt by rinsing.

IT MAKES ABOUT 7 CUPS

- 1 pound cauliflower broken into florets
- ½ pound scarlet runner beans trimmed
- ½ pound green tomatoes, cut into chunks
- 1 pound shallots, peeled and halved if small
- 6 cups of diced marrow squash flesh
- ⅞ cup of salt
- 6¾ cups of malt vinegar
- ⅞ cup of sugar
- One rounded tbsp of English mustard powder
- 2 tsp mustard seeds
- 1 tsp ground ginger
- Four small dried chilies, crushed
- ¼ round cup of cornstarch
- 2 tbsp turmeric

PICCALILLI

Homegrown, seasonal veggies can be preserved well with piccalilli, and the mix can be altered depending on the season. Another clever method is to use up marrow squash, or you can use zucchini instead. Both crops frequently fall into the "feast or famine" category; there is typically an abundance while available.

1. Mix all the vegetables, put them in a bowl with salt sprinkled in between, and let them overnight. The following day, drain the vegetables again after giving them a thorough rinse to remove all the salt.
2. Add the vinegar to the pan with the sugar, mustard powder, seeds, ginger, and dried chiles. The vegetables should be added and simmered until barely soft but with some crunch. Depending on your pickle texture, you can steam the vegetables until mushy or leave them crisp.
3. Stir in a few tbsp of the pan's vinegar, cornstarch, and turmeric, then boil the mixture for two to three minutes.
4. Piccalilli should be poured into hot, sterilized jars, cooled, and sealed.

MAKES ABOUT 3 CUPS

- 2 pounds shallots
- ½ (rounded) cup of salt
- 2⅓ cups of pickling vinegar

PICKLED SHALLOTS

Pickled onions are a traditional British pickle favorite among kids and adults. They work well with just about anything, but pickled onions, a slice of crusty bread, and a wedge of sharp cheese are tough to top for a quick lunch. Your onions must be brined for a few days to preserve their original crunch before being put into jars and coated with seasoned vinegar. A few jars of this pickle should always be kept on the pantry shelf because, aside from that, it has to be the simplest pickle there is.

1. Shallots should not be peeled before being placed in a big bowl. Pour the brine over the shallots and let it sit for 12 hours after dissolving half the salt in a quart of water. Shallots are drained and skinned.
2. Use the remaining salt and the same amount of water to make a second brine, then pour it over the shallots and let it sit for two to three days.
3. While waiting for the bringing period to end, if you don't already have pickling vinegar steeping in a cabinet, make a batch of the short version and let it sit until it is cold.
4. The onions should be salted off, rinsed, and snacked into sterilized jars. Cover them entirely by pouring the cold pickling vinegar over them. Seal the jars with a lid. After bottling, the shallots will continue to be flavorful and crisp for up to 6 months.

SWEET & SOUR ONIONS

To give this pickle a delicious sweet and sour tang, sweeter vinegar than that used in the preceding recipe. Making it is pretty simple.

In this case, sweet pickling vinegar is used for pickling the onions. Use the preceding recipe as directed, but use some sweet pickling vinegar already steeping in a cabinet or prepare some speedier substitutes.

SWEET KOSHER DILL PICKLES

These are the specific favorites in my family. I prepare jars after cucumbers as long as my garden's supply lasts. We eat them with everything, but our preferred meal is a sandwich. Eating homemade bread with grilled ham, cheese, and pickles is delicious.

YIELD: APPROX. 9 QUARTS

- 16 cups of water
- 4½ cups of sugar
- 4 cups of white vinegar
- Two tsp salt
- 1½ packages Mrs. Wages Kosher Dill Pickles mix
- 2 gallons of cucumbers, sliced

1. Mix Mrs. Wages, water, sugar, white vinegar, and salt in a large stockpot.
2. Heat on medium-low until the sugar and seasoning mix is dissolved and the mixture begins to boil.
3. While the brine is heating, wash and slice the cucumbers.
4. Fill the clean, prepared jars with cucumbers, careful not to overfill them. To help the cucumbers settle, I fill them and give them a few sharp slaps on the counters. There should be one inch of headspace allowed to accommodate brine.
5. Before adding the brine to the cucumbers, ensure your canner is hot and ready to process the pickles.
6. Using a funnel, carefully pour the hot brine into the prepared jars, leaving a headspace of 1 inch.
7. Remove any sticky brine residue by wiping the jar rims and lids.
8. Put the lids on the clean jars using the screw bands that are included.

9. Place the jars inside the canner using a jar lifter, ensuring they are completely submerged.
10. Add the pickles and cook for 5 minutes once the water has reached a rolling boil.
11. After removing it from the canner, set it aside for 24 hours on a solid surface. After 24 hours, your jars are prepared to be kept. I permanently remove the screw bands before storing them because I need them for my future canning endeavor.

BREAD-AND-BUTTER PICKLES

Although the extra onions make these pickles slightly sweeter than the kosher dill type, they go well with sandwiches.

YIELD: APPROX. 5 QUARTS

- 1 gallon thinly sliced cucumbers
- 2 cups of thinly sliced onions
- ¼ cup of salt
- 4 cups of sugar
- 2 cups of white vinegar
- 1½ cups of water
- One tsp turmeric
- One tsp of celery seed

1. Mix the salt, cucumbers, and onions.
2. Thoroughly drain after 3 hours of soaking.
3. Bring the sugar, vinegar, water, turmeric, and celery seed to a moderate boil over medium heat.
4. Fill the clean, prepared jars with the cucumber-onion mixture; be careful not to overfill them. To help the cucumbers settle, I fill them and give them a few sharp slaps on the counters. There should be one inch of headspace allowed to accommodate brine.
5. Before adding the brine to the cucumbers, ensure your canner is ready to process the pickles and filled with boiling water.
6. Using a funnel, carefully pour the hot brine into the prepared jars, leaving a headspace of 1 inch.

7. Wipe the jars and rims, removing any sticky brine residue.
8. Screw on the jar lids using the screw bands that came with the clean jars.
9. Place the jars inside the canner using a jar lifter, ensuring they are entirely covered by water.
10. Add the pickles and cook for 5 minutes after the water has reached a rolling boil.
11. Take out of the canner, and set aside for 24 hours on a firm surface. After 24 hours, your jars are prepared to be kept. I permanently remove the screw bands before storing them because I need them for my future canning endeavor.

MUSTARD PICKLES

These pickles make a delicious accent to a cheese or veggie tray.

YIELD: APPROX. 4 QUARTS

- 1½ cups of white vinegar
- 3 cups of water
- 1 tbsp dry mustard
- 2 cups of sugar
- One tsp of pickling spice
- One tsp salt
- 1 gallon small, whole cucumbers

1. Mix white vinegar, water, dry mustard, sugar, pickling spice, and salt in a large stockpot.
2. Heat the mixture on medium-low until the sugar and seasonings have dissolved, and the sauce begins to boil.
3. While the brine cooks, wash and slice the cucumbers.
4. Fill clean, prepared jars with cucumbers; careful not to overfill them. To help the cucumbers settle, I fill them and give them a few sharp slaps on the counters. There should be one inch of headspace allowed to accommodate brine.
5. Before adding the brine to the cucumbers, ensure your canner is ready to process the pickles and filled with boiling water.

6. Using a funnel, carefully pour the hot brine into the prepared jars, leaving a headspace of 1 inch.
7. Wipe the jars and rims, removing any sticky brine residue.
8. Screw on the jar lids using the screw bands that came with the clean jars.
9. Place the jars inside the canner using a jar lifter, ensuring they are entirely covered by water.
10. Add the pickles and cook for 5 minutes after the water has reached a rolling boil.
11. After removing it from the canner, set it aside for 24 hours on a solid surface. After 24 hours, your jars are prepared to be kept. I permanently remove the screw bands before storing them because I need them for my future canning endeavor.

SWEET DILL PICKLES

Sweet dill pickles taste more like sweet pickles when the kosher dill mix is absent.

YIELD: APPROX. 4 QUARTS

- One tsp of dill seed or one head of fresh dill
- One onion, sliced
- One clove of garlic
- 2 cups of water
- 3 cups of sugar
- 2 cups of vinegar
- 2 tbsp salt
- 1-gallon cucumbers

1. Heat the water, sugar, vinegar, and salt in a large stockpot until the sugar dissolves and the mixture boils.
2. While the brine is heating, wash and slice the cucumbers.
3. Fill clean, prepared jars with cucumbers, careful not to overfill them. To help the cucumbers settle, I fill them and give them a few sharp slaps on the counters. Include one onion, one clove of garlic, one fresh dill head, one tsp,
4. Before adding the brine to the cucumbers, ensure your canner is ready to process the pickles and filled with boiling water.

5. Using a funnel, carefully pour the warm brine into the jars, leaving 1 inch of headroom.
6. Wipe the jars and rims, removing any sticky brine residue.
7. Attach the screw bands with the pots to the clean jars' lids to keep them closed.
8. Place the jars inside the canner using a jar lifter, ensuring they are entirely covered by water.
9. While preparing pickles, boil water for five minutes.
10. Take the food from the canner and let it rest for 24 hours on a stable surface. After 24 hours, your jars are prepared to be kept. I permanently remove the screw bands before storing them because I need them for my future canning endeavor.

BANANA PICKLES

A typical Amish pickle frequently served for lunch following church is banana pickles. They are taken from large cucumbers and chopped into spears.

YIELD: APPROX. 6 QUARTS

- 2 cups of vinegar
- 2 cups of water
- 6 cups of sugar
- Two tsp salt
- Two tsp of celery seed
- Two tsp turmeric
- Two tsp of mustard seed
- 1 gallon large pared, deseeded cucumber spears

1. Mix the vinegar, water, sugar, salt, celery seed, turmeric, and mustard in a sizable stockpot.
2. Until the mixture begins to boil and the sugar and seasonings have dissolved, heat on medium-low.
3. While the brine is heating, get the cucumbers ready.
4. Fill the clean, prepared jars with cucumbers; be careful not to overfill them. To help the cucumbers settle, I fill them and give them a few sharp slaps on the counters. There should be one inch of headspace allowed to accommodate brine.

5. Before adding the brine to the cucumbers, ensure your canner is hot and ready to process the pickles.
6. Using a funnel, carefully pour the hot brine into the prepared jars, leaving a headspace of 1 inch.
7. Remove any sticky brine residue by wiping the jar rims and lids.
8. Put the lids on the clean jars using the screw bands that are included.
9. Place the jars inside the canner using a jar lifter, ensuring they are completely submerged.
10. Add the pickles and cook for 5 minutes once the water has reached a rolling boil.
11. Please remove the canner, and leave it to rest for 24 hours on a firm surface. After 24 hours, your jars are prepared to be kept. I permanently remove the screw bands before storing them because I need them for my future canning endeavor.

REFRIGERATOR PICKLES

There is no can for these pickles. After being cut into slices and doused in brine, they are cooled. They may be stored in the refrigerator for up to 30 days and are a great way to use extra cucumbers.

YIELD: APPROX. 2 QUARTS

- 7–9 cups of sliced cucumbers
- 1 cup of sliced green peppers
- 1 cup thinly sliced onion
- 2 tbsp salt
- 1 tbsp celery seed
- 1 cup of white vinegar
- 2 cups of sugar

1. Sliced cucumbers are put in a large bowl.
2. Add the peppers and onions.
3. Add salt and celery seed to vegetables before serving.
4. Mix vinegar and sugar and stir until sugar dissolves.
5. After thoroughly stirring, add the mixture to the vegetables.
6. Keep in the refrigerator and eat within 30 days.

PICKLED VEGETABLES

CRISP DILLY GREEN BEANS

Dilly beans and pickles are comparable. On the other hand, jelly beans feel different. They taste even better on a hot summer day when served ice cold as a side dish for barbecues.

YIELD: APPROX. 4 PINTS

- 2 pounds small, tender green beans
- 1 tsp cayenne pepper
- Four cloves garlic
- Four large heads dill
- 2 cups of water
- ¼ cup of salt
- 1-pint white vinegar

1. Remove the stems from the green beans and pack them into jars with ½ -inch headspace.
2. Fill every jar with one head of dill, garlic clove, and ¼ tsp cayenne pepper.
3. Bring water, vinegar, and salt to a boil.
4. Add brine to the beans, allowing a 1-inch headspace.
5. Wipe the jars and rims, removing any sticky brine residue.
6. Screw on the jar lids using the screw bands that came with the clean jars.
7. Place the jars inside the canner using a jar lifter, ensuring they are entirely covered by water.
8. Once the water reaches a rolling boil, process the green beans for five minutes.
9. Take the food from the canner and let it rest for 24 hours on a stable surface. After 24 hours, your jars are prepared to be kept. I permanently remove the screw bands before storing them because I need them for my future canning endeavor.

PICKLED BEETS

Pickled beets are another classic Amish supper consumed following church sessions. The taste of these beets is sweet and bitter.

YIELD: APPROX. 10 PINTS

- 10 pounds fresh, raw beets
- 2 cups of vinegar
- 2 cups of water or liquid from cooking beets (beet juice)
- 2 cups of sugar
- 1 tsp salt

1. Clean the beets thoroughly.
2. Keep the stem tips intact but cut off the leafy stem tops. Later, the shelters would be taken off. Don't remove the root end, either.
3. Put the beets in a big stockpot, add water to cover, and simmer for about an hour or until fork-tender.
4. Two cups of cooking liquid should be set aside for the brine.
5. Allow the beets to cool until they are manageable.
6. Trim the beets' tops, and root ends, then use your fingers to peel them. Don't cut through the sides of the beets.
7. Slice or chop the beets, then add the pieces to jars, leaving 1 inch of headspace.
8. Slightly bring to a boil the remaining ingredients and cooking liquid.
9. Before adding the brine to the beets, ensure your canner is loaded with boiling water and prepared to process the beets.
10. Slowly pour the hot brine into the prepared jars using a funnel, leaving a headspace of ½ inches.
11. Wipe the jars and rims, removing any sticky brine residue.
12. Screw on the jar lids using the screw bands that come with the clean jars.
13. Make sure the jars are fully submerged in water before inserting them into the canner using a jar lifter.
14. Bring water to a roaring boil, then process beets for 20 minutes.
15. Take the food out of the canner and let it sit for 24 hours on a stable surface. After 24 hours, your jars are prepared to be kept. I permanently remove the screw bands before storing them because I need them for my future canning endeavor.

HARVARD BEETS

Whether served as a fast vegetable, almost any meal pairs well with this beet.

YIELD: APPROX. 4 PINTS

- 1½ cups of sugar
- 2½ tbsp cornstarch
- 2½ tsp salt
- ½ cup of vinegar
- ¾ cup of water
- 8 cups of cooked beets, sliced

1. Mix the cornstarch, sugar, and salt.
2. Add vinegar and water.
3. Stir slowly.
4. Over medium heat, bring the brine to a boil while stirring frequently.
5. After removing the beets from the heat, add the brine.
6. Pour into the jars.
7. Wipe the jars and rims, removing any sticky brine residue.
8. Screw on the jar lids using the screw bands that came with the clean jars.
9. Place the jars inside the canner using a jar lifter, ensuring they are entirely covered by water.
10. After bringing the water to a full boil, add the beets and process for 10 minutes.
11. Take out of the canner, and set aside for 24 hours on a firm surface. After 24 hours, your jars are prepared to be kept. I permanently remove the screw bands before storing them because I need them for my future canning endeavor.

CHEESE

On early Pennsylvanian farms, creating cheese came naturally. For their own dairy needs, most families had a few cows. They incorporated the leftover milk into the mixes for cookies and cakes. However, the cook created cheese when the supply of sour milk exceeded the demand. She applied a custom she had acquired in Europe and made schmierkase, egg cheese, ball cheese, and a cup of cheese here.

There were still frequent occasions when milk was available to produce cheese, even as dairying grew in eastern Pennsylvania. A senior woman recalls that the milk company we sell to didn't haul on Sundays when we started the farm. We would have several full milk cans over the summer because we couldn't ship that milk, and I would use that to create cheese. I mostly made it for our family.

Schmierkase was served during Sunday lunch after the church service along the way. There was frequently more cheese spread available than jam or jelly. We didn't always eat that at church. We wouldn't be able to have it if the cows dried up! However, it started to appear on the Sunday lunch menu very frequently.

But even among the Amish, once routine, things continue to change. A young Amish woman said, "There is a problem now with getting the crumbs to create the cheese. The cause? "I don't know any Amish folks that only have a few cows right now. They only have one cow and need more milk to be sour for cheese, or they have a dairy and ship all their milk. My source for cheese curds is a Mennonite woman whose family does own a few cows. She uses the extra milk they don't drink to make crumbs.

The cheese crumbs are sold in one or two local shops, but the Amish, who traditionally make their own, think the cost could be more manageable. They therefore adjust. We melt the processed orange American cheese for church with margarine, ordinary milk, and evaporated milk. A middle-aged woman said, "It tastes almost like the old schmierkase. An older man said, "We usually eat peanut butter blended with margarine and something creamy like a marshmallow in the church district where I belong. It spreads quickly and could be more affluent.

Even though they are only occasionally on the cook's menu nowadays, here are the recipes for four traditional favorites.

SCHMIERKASE

- 2½ gallons of milk, skimmed of its cream
- 2 tsp. baking soda
- 1¼–1½ cups of warm water
- ⅓ cup of butter
- 2 tsp. salt
- 1 cup of hot water
- Let milk sour until it becomes thick, then heat to 115°–120°.

1. Pour half of the milk into a bag made of coarse cotton. Squeeze as much liquid out as you can. Crumble curds after adding them to a bowl. With the leftover milk, repeat the operation.
2. Allow crumbs to age for two to three days at room temperature (up to 5 days if a more robust flavor is desired).
3. Mix well with baking soda to the crumbs (around 4 cups). Add 1¼–1½ cups of warm water after pouring it into the double boiler and letting it sit for 30 minutes.
4. Stirring continuously, bring to a boil. Add the butter, salt, and boiling water, 1¼ cup.
5. Cook, stirring to mix crumbs, for 10 to 12 minutes. Spread on toast, then let the mixture cool.

IT MAKES ABOUT 1½ QUARTS OF CHEESE

COTTAGE CHEESE

- 1½ gallons milk
- 1 tsp. salt
- ½ cup of fresh cream

1. Till the milk becomes quite thick, let it sour. Heat to 115° to 120°, then place in a sack made of coarse fabric and let drain overnight.
2. When curds are dried, shred until powdery and ultimately include salt.
3. When ready to serve, add the fresh cream and thoroughly blend.

IT MAKES ABOUT 3½ CUPS OF CHEESE

EGG CHEESE

- 2 quarts of new milk
- Five eggs
- 2 cups of buttermilk or sour milk
- 1 tsp. salt
- 1 tsp. sugar

1. Bring fresh milk to a rolling boil.
2. To achieve a lemon color, beat the eggs. Add salt, sugar, buttermilk, or soured milk. Just combine, then carefully pour into the hot, fresh milk. For five minutes, cover and leave in place.
3. As the curds and whey separate, stir the mixture. Lift the curds into a mold with drainage holes on the bottom using a slotted spoon. Softly layer the curds into the mold to keep the cheese from packing tightly. When thoroughly chilled, the cheese can be unmolded onto a dish or cut out of the container and used as a spread on bread.

CUP OF CHEESE

- 2½ gallons milk
- 1½ tsp. baking soda
- 1½ tsp. salt
- ½ cup of water

1. Till the milk becomes quite thick, let it sour. Pour into a thick cloth bag after heating to 120 degrees, and let drain overnight.
2. Cheese and soda should be combined appropriately after the curds have crumbled finely. Place in a bowl, cover with a cloth, and let sit for three days at room temperature. Every morning and night, stir.
3. After the third day, put the cheese bowl in the top section of a double boiler. Add salt and water and whisk till smooth overheat. Cheese should be pungently scented, thick, and yellow.
4. Pour the mixture into cups. Spread the cooled mixture on toast to serve. Before eating the cheese, some people like to sprinkle molasses or honey over it.

BEVERAGES

The arrival of a delegation from the kitchen with ice-cold lemonade and peppermint water brightens steamy hot days in the hay fields.

Fresh meadow tea is the perfect reward for gardening in the late afternoon.

Dark summer nights are spent with pretzels and homemade root beer.

Apple cider is a sign of cooler days.

Most Amish women are inventive cooks who still rely on their crops and orchards to produce refreshments for their families. Lemons and root beer mix are grocery store purchases, but other than those two ingredients, conventional preparations start from scratch.

FRESH MEADOW TEA

In eastern Pennsylvania, many different types of tea are growing in meadows, gardens, and flowerbeds. You can use the leaves fresh, dried, or frozen.

Many chefs store a gallon jar of fresh tea in the fridge from May through September. Additionally, they make sure that tea stems and leaves are spread out on paper in a seldom-used room of the house to dry. (It's a strategy to ensure meadow tea will always be available for hot winter drinks.) When time or the season prevents making tea with fresh leaves, those with access to freezers have discovered the simplicity of preparing a tea concentrate and freezing it for some future times.

- 1 cup of sugar
- 1-pint water
- 1 cup of fresh tea leaves, either peppermint or spearmint
- juice of 1 lemon
- water

1. Bring sugar and one pint of water to a boil while stirring constantly.
2. Tea leaves should be covered with boiling syrup and steeped for 20 minutes. Once the tea has cooled, remove the leaves.
3. Add enough water to produce a half-gallon of tea and lemon juice.
4. Whether hot or cold, serve.

MAKES ½ GALLON

FROZEN MEADOW TEA CONCENTRATE

- 2 cups of sugar
- 5 cups of water
- One large handful of garden tea
- 1 cup of lemon juice
- 1 cup of orange juice
- Water

1. Boil 5 cups of water with sugar. Add garden tea on top. For one hour, cover and steep.
2. Take tea out. Insert juices. Freeze.

IT MAKES ABOUT 6 QUARTS

ROOT BEER

- 1 tsp. dry yeast
- ½ cup of warm water
- 2 cups of granulated sugar
- 1-quart hot water
- Four tsp. Root beer extract

1. Mix yeast with 1 cup of warm water.
2. In one quart of hot water, dissolve the sugar.
3. Mix sugar, dissolved yeast, and root beer essence in a gallon jar. Warm water should be added to the pot, and the components should be thoroughly mixed.
4. Jar lid on. Spend four hours in the warm sun. The following day, the root beer will be consumable. Before serving, chill.

MAKES 1-GALLON ROOT BEER

LEMONADE

Never mind that Pennsylvania's orchards didn't have lemon trees. A woman in her fifties says, "When I was a girl, we bought lemons at the store." In the summer, we always had lemons on hand for lemonade. The fruit added variety to the selection of hot-weather drinks because it was relatively affordable and easily accessible.

- Four lemons
- 3 cups of sugar
- 1-quart hot water
- 3 quarts of cold water

1. Slice and clean lemons. Delete the seeds. Use a potato masher to mix sugar and lemon slices thoroughly.
2. Add boiling water to the lemon and sugar mixture, whisk to dissolve the sugar, and extract the lemon pulp and juice.
3. Before discarding lemon slices, squeeze a few pieces by hand to extract the remaining juice. The mixture should be thoroughly mixed after adding cold water. Cool, then serve.

MAKES 1 GALLON

GRAPE JUICE CONCENTRATE

Many Amish farms have Concord grape vines that grow on arbors and fences.

Fresh grape juice is provided throughout the season; it is canned, frequently in concentrated form, and served on special occasions throughout the year.

- 10 lbs. grapes
- 2 cups of water
- 1½ lbs. sugar

1. After washing, add water and simmer grapes until tender. Fruit should be put through a press until the juice stops pouring.
2. Stir in the sugar until it is dissolved.
3. Juice should be heated up before being poured into bottles and jars—process for 10 minutes in a hot bath.

EGGNOG

Eggnog does not have to be reserved for the holiday season when plenty of eggs, milk, and cream are available. According to a well-known chef, "We cooked eggnog rather frequently. We consumed it more regularly throughout the year than during the holidays when other treats were available. Of course, we had milk and eggs, and since my father suffered from stomach ulcers, he drank eggnog.

- Four eggs
- ⅓ cup of granulated sugar
- ⅛ tsp. nutmeg
- dash of salt
- 4 Tbsp. lemon juice. Apple cider vinegar mixed with 2 Tbsp. water
- 4 cups of cold milk
- ½ cup of cold cream

1. The thickening of the eggs. Add sugar, seasonings, and vinegar or lemon juice.
2. Beat till foamy after adding the cream and chilled milk. Serve right away.

MAKES SIX LARGE CUPS

PEPPERMINT DRINK

Cooks created vinegar punch, soda water, and peppermint drink to prevent the farmhands from dehydrating during the sweltering summer days in the field. More so than fruit beverages, the chemical concoctions relieved thirst and soothed overheated stomachs.

- 2 quarts of ice water
- ½ cup of sugar

1. A couple of drops of peppermint or peppermint spirits essence
2. Mix all items thoroughly. Serve chilled.

MAKES EIGHT SERVINGS

TOMATO JUICE COCKTAIL

This rich, flavorful beverage has added to the benefits of growing tomatoes. The fruit is a mainstay in the Amish diet and is consumed in various ways, including fresh slices, stewed versions, baked goods, and soup.

This basic dish can be used in a variety of healthy ways. It can be consumed as an appetizer or a snack and as the foundation for a flavorful soup.

- ½ bushel tomatoes
- Three stalks celery
- Three large onions
- Six medium carrots
- Three green peppers
- a little water
- 1 cup of sugar
- 2 Tbsp. salt

1. 1" piece of raw veggies should be cut. Place everything in a big stockpot. Add water until it is 1 inch deep. Cook gently till tender, then press through.
2. Add sugar and salt to the blended mixture. Up to a boil. Place in jars. Process for 40 minutes in a hot bath.

SPICED CIDER

Commercial cider presses were started to accommodate the demand for cider production. From Pennsylvania's central counties eastward, the landscape is covered in family orchards and small-scale fruit farms.

The apple beverage is often served cold, but in recent years it has gained popularity as a hot beverage, especially when winter approaches and the cider season comes to a close.

- 1-gallon apple cider
- 1 cup of orange juice
- 1 Tbsp. lemon juice
- Three cinnamon sticks
- 1 tsp. allspice

- 1 tsp. ground cloves
- sugar as needed

1. All ingredients—sugar excluded—should be combined. If necessary, taste and add sugar.
2. For 6 to 8 minutes, gently simmer after bringing to a boil. Serve heated after straining.

MAKES 16-17 CUPS OF CIDER

PUDDINGS, DUMPLINGS, AND DESSERTS

Most Amish people put in much effort and live orderly, modest lifestyles. However, they like delicious food and consume sweets practically carelessly. Although pie will undoubtedly always be a favorite, it has some fierce rivals in apple dumplings, cracker pudding, and stewed rhubarb.

A cook in charge of three full meals daily wants to expand her menu, make tasty cuisine, and feed the crowd. So whether it's a lunchtime soup and sandwich or a hearty meat and potatoes dinner, there will undoubtedly be a substantial dessert.

Suppers can be made entirely of some of these foods because of their historical significance and widespread affection. For instance, apple rolls, with their dough resembling dumplings, probably originated from the traditionally cooked puddings that were frequently consumed in early Pennsylvania in bowls of milk. 7 The "pap," or cornstarch pudding, was the foundation for numerous snack meals.

The flavors of many of these recipes come from fruit or readily available extracts, such as vanilla. Others are constructed around crackers, practically required in an Amish diet. Usually, eggs and milk are present in the mix or, at the very least, in the eating.

These traditional dishes can be served as a standalone dessert for regular family meals. They are typically filled with pie and cake when guests are at the table.

VANILLA CORNSTARCH PUDDING

Although vanilla was the most common flavor, some cooks thrilled their families by placing a dollop of chocolate directly in the middle of the complete serving dish. A middle-aged woman recalls that her mother would keep some pudding, mix it with chocolate syrup, and spoon it into the middle to give everything a little more taste.

The ideal temperature at which cornstarch should be served varies depending on preferences. Some people insist that it be heated. Some people are passionate about eating it cold, too. The first round is served hot when the batch is more significant than required; the leftovers are chilled.

- 1-quart fresh milk
- ⅔ cup of granulated sugar
- ⅓ cup of cornstarch
- dash of salt
- Two eggs, beaten
- ¼ cup of milk
- 1 tsp. vanilla

1. In the top of the double boiler, scald 1 quart of milk. Mix the sugar, cornstarch, salt, eggs, and ¼ cup of milk. Add the smooth mixture to the hot milk and whisk continuously while cooking until thickened.
2. Add vanilla after removing it from the heat.

MAKES 8–10 SERVINGS

CHOCOLATE CORNSTARCH PUDDING

- 3 Tbsp. cornstarch
- ⅓ cup of sugar
- ½ tsp salt
- 3 Tbsp. cocoa
- 2 cups of milk
- 1 tsp. vanilla

1. Well-blended dry ingredients Heat ½ cup of milk in a pot. Add the remaining ½ cup of milk to the dry ingredients and whisk until smooth.

2. Stir the moistened dry ingredients into the heated milk before a skin forms. Stir continuously while the mixture is heated until it thickens and gently boils (it should not boil vigorously). Remove from heat, and then either serve warm.

MAKES 4–6 SERVINGS

CRACKER PUDDING

The ritual of eating cracker pudding was enjoyable. Saltines can now be added to the diet in another way, even if the finished dessert hardly even notices their presence.

The eastern Pennsylvanian Amish had access to coconuts even seventy-five years ago. One over 80 years old says, "We would buy a whole one and grate it ourselves."

- Two eggs separated
- ⅔ cup of granulated sugar
- 1-quart milk
- 1¼–1½ cups of saltine crackers, coarsely broken
- ¾ cup of coconut, grated
- 1 tsp. vanilla
- 3 Tbsp. sugar

1. Together, sugar and egg yolks are beaten—heat after pouring into a pot. Add the milk gradually while stirring continuously.
2. Coconut and crackers are then cooked until thickened. Add vanilla after removing it from the heat.
3. Put into the baking pan. Beat the egg whites with 3 tbsp of sugar until they are stiff. Spread the meringue over the pudding and then toast it under the broiler.

MAKES 6–8 SERVINGS

GRAHAM CRACKER PUDDING

- A pudding of particular delight to children!
- 16 whole graham crackers
- ¼ cup of granulated sugar
- ¼ cup of butter or margarine, melted
- Four tsp. Flour
- ½ cup of + 2 Tbsp. sugar

- 2 cups of milk
- Three eggs separated
- ½ tsp. vanilla

1. Break up Graham crackers. Mix with butter and ¼ cup of sugar. Create fine crumbs by mixing. In the bottom and edges of the baking dish, press ¾ of the crumb mixture. Save any leftover crumbs.
2. Mix the flour and ½ cup of sugar—the milk- within the top of a double boiler. Bring to a boil—mix beaten egg yolks with ½ cup of the heated milk mixture. Refill the cup with the remaining hot milk and reheat to boiling. Stirring continuously; cook for 2-3 minutes. Add vanilla after removing it from the heat. Add to a plate lined with crackers.
3. Egg whites should be stiffened up. Add the final 2 Tbsp. of sugar gradually. Top the pudding with beaten egg whites. Add the saved cracker crumbs on top. The meringue should be caramelized after 5-8 minutes of baking at 350°; before serving, cool.

MAKES 8-10 SERVING

BANANA PUDDING

As stated above, make Graham Cracker Pudding. Pour one-third of the custard into the plate with the crackers. Add sliced bananas on top. Layers of pudding and bananas should continue to alternate. Meringue and a scattering of the saved cracker crumbs complete the dish.

MAKES 8-10 SERVINGS

TAPIOCA PUDDING

A long time ago, making tapioca pudding was not an impulse decision. One elderly woman says, "We used the big pearl tapioca that had to soak overnight." Yet another adds, "We ate a lot of tapioca pudding."

- 4 cups of milk
- ⅓ cup of minute tapioca
- Two eggs separated
- ½ cup of sugar
- pinch of salt

- ½ tsp. Vanilla or lemon extract

In a large saucepan, mix the milk and tapioca. Cook the tapioca while frequently stirring until it is transparent.

Egg yolks are beaten with sugar and salt. To egg yolks, add ½ cup of the heated milk mixture. To the remaining heated milk, add this back. Heat once more until boiling. Stirring continuously; cook for two minutes. Get rid of the heat.

Add the seasoning and stiffly beaten egg whites—place in serving bowls.

IT MAKES ABOUT TEN SERVINGS

APPLE DUMPLINGS

These apple "pies" can be served as a substantial dessert or meal in individual containers. The best way to consume them is warm with cold milk on top.

- Eight apples, cored and pared
- 3 cups of flour
- 1 tsp. salt
- 1¼ cups of shortening
- One egg, beaten
- ⅓ cup of cold water
- 1 Tbsp. vinegar
- ½ cup of margarine
- 1 cup of brown sugar
- 4 Tbsp. water

1. Mix salt and flour. Shortening is cut in.
2. Stir the egg, vinegar, and ⅓ cup of cold water into the shortening mixture. Give it some time to stand.
3. On a floured surface, roll out the dough and cut it into considerable squares to encircle an apple. Once thoroughly covered in dough, place an apple on a greased 9" x 13" baking sheet.
4. Boil 4 tbsp water, brown sugar, and margarine. Douse dumplings in liquid.
5. Dumplings should be baked at 350° for 40–50 minutes or until golden brown.

MAKES EIGHT SERVINGS

APPLE ROLLS

The apple dumpling version was offered as a main course or a lighter supper. A young Amish mother recalls, "We occasionally ate it with potatoes to make it more substantial." It reminds me of a tasty cinnamon roll,

- 4 cups of flour
- 2 Tbsp. granulated sugar
- 2 Tbsp. baking powder
- 1 tsp. salt
- 2½ Tbsp. shortening
- One egg
- Milk

1. Sliced, cored, and peeled apples, six medium-sized
2. assemble the dry ingredients. Once the mixture resembles small peas, gradually add shortening.
3. After beating an egg in a cup, add milk. Till dough forms, mix into the crumbs.
4. Roll to a thickness of ¼". Add apple slices on top. Cut into 1" pieces after rolling up like a jelly roll. Lay in a greased baking dish, cover with hot syrup, and bake for 35 to 40 minutes at 375 degrees. Milk should be served warm.

MAKES 6–8 SERVINGS

SYRUP

- 2 cups of brown sugar
- 2 cups of water
- ¼ cup of butter or margarine
- 2 Tbsp. flour

1. Together, blend. Stirring constantly, bring to a boil—3 minutes of simmering. Add to apple rolls.

BAKED APPLES

Dessert-like yet lighter than dumplings or a cobbler. Eat hot out of the oven with milk, whipped cream,

Additionally, these apples go well with fried potatoes, scrapple, mush, and eggs.

- 8–10 apples, cored, peeled, and cut in half
- ¾ cup of granulated sugar
- ¾ cup of brown sugar
- ½ cup of flour
- 1 tsp. cinnamon
- 2 tsp. butter or margarine melted
- 1 cup of water

1. Fill a 9" x 13" baking pan with apples after greasing it.
2. The following ingredients should be combined in a pot in the order listed before boiling. Stirring often, simmer until thick.
3. When the apples are soft, bake with syrup for 30-45 minutes at 350 degrees.

MAKES 8–10 SERVINGS

BAKED EGG CUSTARD

- Six eggs
- 6 Tbsp. sugar
- dash of salt
- 1 Tbsp. vanilla
- 1-quart milk

1. After beating the eggs, add the sugar, salt, and vanilla.
2. Slowly include scalded milk into the egg mixture. Stir it well to mix everything.
3. Pour into a baking pan or custard cups—place in a pan of hot water as high as the custard level.
4. A knife inserted in the center of the custard should come out clean after 40 minutes of baking at 325 degrees.

MAKES EIGHT SERVINGS

CARAMEL PUDDING

One elder woman recalls her grandma cooking this for supper when her family hosted the church service.

"Grussmommy frequently cooked caramel pudding even though she had no idea how many people she would serve. With ground peanuts on top, I adore it. Daddy is still there, shelling the peanuts for the top, and I can still see him. It was always served cold by Grussmommy.

- 2 Tbsp. butter
- ¾ cup of brown sugar
- 1-quart milk
- Two eggs
- 2 Tbsp. cornstarch
- 2 Tbsp. flour
- pinch of salt
- ¼ cup of milk
- chopped peanuts

1. Butter should be melted in a large saucepan. Stir in the brown sugar after adding it. One quart of milk should be heated before being stirred in.
2. Mix eggs, cornstarch, flour, salt, and ¼ cup of milk together. Before it reaches boiling point, add to the warm milk and continue stirring. With a rotary beater, remove from heat. Before serving, let the top be incredible, and then top with freshly chopped peanuts.

MAKES EIGHT SERVINGS

COTTAGE PUDDING

This cake has a name that refers to the cake-like puddings frequently served with fruit and milk and steamed or boiled in 19th-century America.

It might belong to the shortcake family now.

- ¼ cup of butter, margarine, or shortening
- ⅔ cup of granulated sugar

- One egg, well beaten
- 1 tsp. vanilla
- 2½ cups of flour
- Four tsp. Baking powder
- ½ tsp. salt
- 1 cup of milk

1. Shortening and sugar are combined. Egg and vanilla should be thoroughly mixed in.
2. Sift the dry ingredients together, then add them to the creamed batter in alternating batches with the milk. Avoid over-stirring.
3. Thirty-five minutes at 350 degrees in an 8" square cake pan that has been buttered.
4. Serve with milk and fruit.

MAKES EIGHT SERVINGS

DATE PUDDING

This moist, decadent dessert is more frequently consumed in Ohio Amish communities than Pennsylvania Amish towns. It was passed on to the settlements further west by their neighbors. The Amish like the cake's chewy sweetness because it has a dried fruit base.

- 1 cup of boiling water
- 1 cup of dates, cut up,
- ½ cup of granulated sugar
- ½ cup of brown sugar
- One egg
- 2 Tbsp. butter or margarine softened
- 1½ cups of flour
- 1 tsp. baking powder
- 1 tsp. Baking soda
- ½ tsp. salt
- 1 cup of nuts, chopped

1. Dates should be covered in boiling water and left to cool.

2. Butter or margarine, eggs, and sugars are creamed together.
3. Then, add the dry ingredients to the batter that has been creamed. Add dates and nuts and stir.
4. Pour into an 11" x 7" x 1½" oiled baking pan. Add sauce on top, then bake at 350° for 40–45 minutes. If preferred, top with whipped cream and serve warm or cold.

MAKES 6–8 SERVINGS

RELISHES

It would help if you always had relishes in your pantry or cellar. They are excellent with grilled meats, sandwiches, hot dogs, and hamburgers. Relishes require a slightly different technique than pickles, although it is still possible. Even though making condiments involves much chopping, I like doing it!

GREEN TOMATO RELISH

This is a fantastic dish to use up any excess green tomatoes when the summer is over.

YIELD: APPROX. 12 PINTS

- 24 large green tomatoes
- Six red and green bell peppers
- 12 large onions
- 3 tbsp celery seed
- 3 tbsp mustard seed
- 1 tbsp salt
- 5 cups of white sugar
- 2 cups of cider vinegar

1. Chop or pulverize the tomatoes, peppers, and onions.
2. Drain in a mesh strainer or colander for one hour.
3. Mix the remaining ingredients with the chopped vegetables in a big stockpot.
4. Boiling takes 4 minutes.
5. Scoop into containers.
6. Process in a hot water bath for 30 minutes.

ONION RELISH

YIELD: APPROX. 3 PINTS

- 14 medium onions
- Six medium green peppers
- Three small hot peppers,
- 4 cups of white vinegar
- 3 cups of sugar
- 2 tbsp salt

1. Cut or mince the onions and peppers.
2. Warm the vinegar, sugar, and salt in a large pot.
3. After coming to a boil, include the vegetables.
4. Simmer for 4 minutes.
5. Transfer to heated jars.
6. Process for ten minutes in a hot water bath.

PEPPER RELISH

YIELD: APPROX. 3 PINTS

- Two dozen large peppers
- 15 medium onions
- ½ cup of salt
- Boiling water (enough to cover vegetables)
- 3 cups of vinegar
- 3 cups of sugar
- 1 tsp mustard seed
- 1 tsp celery seed
- 1 tsp salt

1. Slice or crush the peppers and onions.
2. Sprinkle with salt and then cover with boiling water.
3. Soaking vegetables in boiling water for ten minutes.
4. Well-absorb.
5. Mix vinegar, mustard, celery, salt, and sugar.

6. Pour the vegetables on.
7. Boil for 15 minutes after bringing it to a boil.
8. Fill the hot jars with the mixture, then process for 10 minutes.

PICKLE RELISH

YIELD: APPROX. 15 PINTS

- 4 quarts of cucumbers, chopped
- ¼ cup of salt + 1 tsp salt, divided
- 1 quart onions, chopped
- 1 pint of peppers, chopped
- 2 tsp mustard seed
- 2 tsp celery seed
- 1 tsp turmeric
- 4 cups of sugar
- 2 cups of vinegar

1. Mince or cut the cucumbers.
2. After adding ¼ cup of salt, soak for an hour.
3. Add the remaining vegetables after a thorough drain.
4. Mix celery, mustard, turmeric, and 1 tbsp salt.
5. Pour over the vegetable mixture.
6. Turn the heat to medium and bring to a boil.
7. Simmer for seven minutes.
8. Fill the hot jars with the mixture, then process for 10 minutes.

ZUCCHINI RELISH

This relish takes a little longer to prepare because the vegetables need to soak longer. I've frequently made this relish by merely soaking it for two to three hours, even though the recipe called for overnight soaking, and it still turned out delicious! In my home, this relish is a favorite.

YIELD APPROX. 15 PINTS

- 12 cups of ground or chopped zucchini
- 4 cups of soil

- One large pepper, ground
- 5 tbsp salt
- 2½ cups of vinegar
- 6 cups of sugar
- 1 tbsp dry mustard
- ½ tsp pepper
- ¾ tbsp cornstarch
- ¾ tsp turmeric
- 1½ tsp celery seed

1. Mix salt and the veggie chops.
2. Take a long soak.
3. Completely remove.
4. Mix the remaining ingredients, then drizzle them over the vegetables.
5. Turn the heat to medium and bring to a boil.
6. Simmering for six minutes.
7. Fill heated jars with the mixture, then process for 10 minutes.

.... THE CONCLUSION

Made in the USA
Columbia, SC
01 August 2025